The Visualiser Handbook

The Visualiser Handbook explores how live modelling can be used to break down the barrier between the expert and the student by inviting them to take part in the teacher's thinking process and learn how to do it themselves.

With practical support and examples for all stages of planning and delivering lessons, this guide takes you through how to share your disciplinary expertise with your students via thought narration and structured routines. It shows how you can model thinking, reading and writing tasks in a way that moves students onto increasing levels of independence, builds their metacognitive skills and helps them feel successful and in control of their own thinking as they approach their work. Chapters cover:

- Preparing the classroom and the resources to live model effectively
- Building the conditions – attention and routines
- The 'I do, we do, you do' approach
- Feedback and reflection
- Inclusion and live modelling

Designed for busy teachers and leaders, whether experienced in live modelling or completely new to it, this book is based on evidence and outstanding teaching practice to strengthen your confidence in using this valuable teaching approach.

Chris Webb-Cook is Head of English and Whole School Literacy lead at Ipswich Academy.

The Visualiser Handbook

How to Use Live Modelling to Build Expertise

Chris Webb-Cook

Routledge
Taylor & Francis Group
LONDON AND NEW YORK

Designed cover image: Design © Lisa Dynan

First published 2025
by Routledge
4 Park Square, Milton Park, Abingdon, Oxon OX14 4RN

and by Routledge
605 Third Avenue, New York, NY 10158

Routledge is an imprint of the Taylor & Francis Group, an informa business

© 2025 Chris Webb-Cook

The right of Chris Webb-Cook to be identified as author of this work has been asserted in accordance with sections 77 and 78 of the Copyright, Designs and Patents Act 1988.

All rights reserved. No part of this book may be reprinted or reproduced or utilised in any form or by any electronic, mechanical, or other means, now known or hereafter invented, including photocopying and recording, or in any information storage or retrieval system, without permission in writing from the publishers.

Trademark notice: Product or corporate names may be trademarks or registered trademarks, and are used only for identification and explanation without intent to infringe.

British Library Cataloguing-in-Publication Data
A catalogue record for this book is available from the British Library

Library of Congress Cataloging-in-Publication Data
Names: Webb-Cook, Chris author
Title: The visualiser handbook: how to use live modelling to
build expertise / Chris Webb-Cook.
Description: Abingdon, Oxon; New York, NY: Routledge, 2025. |
Includes bibliographical references and index.
Identifiers: LCCN 2024057891 (print) | LCCN 2024057892 (ebook) |
ISBN 9781032750415 hardback | ISBN 9781032750392 paperback |
ISBN 9781003472261 ebook
Subjects: LCSH: Classroom management | Modeling | Student participation
in administration | Teaching | Educational planning
Classification: LCC LB3013 .W385 2025 (print) |
LCC LB3013 (ebook) | DDC 371.102/4—dc23/eng/20250327
LC record available at https://lccn.loc.gov/2024057891
LC ebook record available at https://lccn.loc.gov/2024057892

ISBN: 978-1-032-75041-5 (hbk)
ISBN: 978-1-032-75039-2 (pbk)
ISBN: 978-1-003-47226-1 (ebk)

DOI: 10.4324/9781003472261

Typeset in Melior
by codeMantra

For Ches and Lottie

Contents

Introduction — 1

Part 1: Why and how

1 What and why — 7
2 Planning and preparation — 10
3 Building the conditions — 17

Part 2: Processes and thought narration

4 I do: reading — 27
5 I do: writing — 36
6 We do – you do: syphoning experience and feeding back — 49

Part 3: Applications

7 Inclusive live modelling: expertise for all — 65
8 Leading live modelling: a thinking and implementation guide — 70
9 The playbook — 78

Bibliography — 83
Index — 85

Introduction

You are good at your subject. You, most probably, have a lovely certificate from a university saying how good you are and might even have been teaching your subject to teenagers for a number of years. You are an expert!

But, what is the nature of this expertise and how can we grow it? As teachers, our job is to know the stuff our students don't (yet). As a gross simplification, our job is to use our expertise to increase theirs: we have to use our subject knowledge and our pedagogies to make experts out of novices. So, the question becomes even more vital; what is the nature of expertise and how do we build it in others?

The acquisition of expertise is a journey from novice, through competence and proficiency to end up at expert and mastery. Much like a lesson, students enter with a gap in their knowledge and/or skills, and they leave with that gap filled to some extent. The novice is able to recognise features but is reliant on rules for structure and support to create. In a lesson, novice students need minute guidance and support. They need sentence starters and extensive support. As students become competent and increasingly proficient, they gain an increased ability to be flexible, to use their broader experiences and deeper knowledge to begin to increase independence. While a student might need sentence starters, they can increasingly manipulate them in a more flexible way. The expert and the master have achieved a depth of experience and knowledge that means they become intuitive and automatic in that area. These are the students who can write with confidence and independence, they need specific guidance, but this is for polish.

The key feature here is the correlation between levels of experience and independence. The simple truth of the education system is that the vast majority of students will find themselves sat in a hall with nothing but a pen and their wits about them at the end of year 11 and year 13. Their independence in interpreting questions and formulating answers will be as important as the amount of knowledge they have. This is why we have teachers, otherwise we would just give them a book, get them to learn it by heart and congratulate ourselves on a job well done. The true measures of an expert are:

- Knowing how to communicate the knowledge they have and selecting a wealth of examples to support specific thoughts and points of view.

- The ability to manipulate knowledge into the correct format and draw conclusions from it.

- The automaticity in completing the processes they use once they have selected the information from their long-term memory.

So, let's return to the fact that we are the experts in our classrooms, we have prepared our lessons and we have selected pedagogical approaches to allow us to impact on our students. We teach them all the things they need to know and then we ask them to show us. We know they know it: we have been covering this material for a week, they have had homework, they aced a low-stakes retrieval quiz and, when we asked them directly with planned and targeted cold calling, they could answer all of our questions. At this point, we are starting to feel smug. So, how come classrooms across the world break into, "How do I start it?" when they have to act with independence? This is where the process of teaching so often breaks down, and I know the challenge of trying not to put my head into my hands. The 'blank page fever' is real and crippling for even our most able learners in the classroom, let alone in assessments and examinations. As teachers, this can be one of the most challenging moments that we face. It can feel like a precipice where the whole lesson could plummet, a high stakes moment, an instant, which, for that child, can make them feel like a success or a failure. It can appear that we have not taught them well or that our carefully laid plans were pointless and it's hard not to feel crestfallen. Realistically, however, we must remember that it is a lack of expertise, not a lack of knowledge that we are facing.

Kennedy called this "the problem of enactment", and it happens in huge numbers of classrooms across the world every single day. Know and do are different. We forget this because we suffer from the 'curse of knowledge'. Our mastery means that enacting is automatic and intuitive, but even at a proficient level of expertise challenging tasks still need structure and clarification. Our students can't hope to reach the level of mastery that we have from years of rigorous training, but we can teach them systems of doing that give them the confidence to act. We can head this issue off and foresee these moments, plan for them and deliver support.

Knowledge-rich curricula, often a focus from government, can forget that knowledge is useless if you don't know how to use it. This 'scientification' of all subjects can be frustrating to teachers in many different disciplines, especially the humanities and the arts. Even scientists struggle to deal with the sheer amount of knowledge content they have to cover! We have to focus on teaching knowledge, but when the final exam is really a test of expertise all that work can come crumbling down if we haven't focussed on increasing the proficiency of our students as writers and thinkers. It is vital to remember: knowledge and expertise *are* different. One is the building, the other the scaffolding that is needed to construct it, but invisible in the finished product. We can give scaffolding in the form of writing frames and sentence starters, but what happens when we are not there to provide these? If we only tell them what to do, but not how to do it we can't be surprised when they can't do it on their own. There comes a point where providing writing frames and sentence starters doesn't solve a problem: it masks one.

We need an approach that we can partner with our existing pedagogies that allows students to share our expertise, to give them insights into the cognitive processes we do automatically. We need to demystify to process by looking at what our expert minds do when they write and show them how they do it to. The answer might well be live modelling.

Live modelling is about teaching and learning in the moment. Live modelling is the pedagogy of demonstration and sharing in collaboration. It's allowing your students into your thought processes to model the expert approach. It's not just what a good one looks like, it's how to make a good one for yourself. It's a step-by-step approach that gives the students the hand and foot holds to climb the mountain of expertise.

Live modelling is so much more than writing an exam style answer under a visualiser, it's an approach to teaching and learning that understands that eventually students are going to have to show their knowledge independently, they are going to have to adapt to different questions deliberately written to push them to the point of failure under high pressure and stress. Teachers need a way to do this without selling out and resorting to teaching to the exam (a pressure we all feel in a world of terminal assessment and high accountability).

However, it is a challenge that takes confidence and effective routines to be successful in the classroom. In a lot of instances, I have spoken to teachers who are nervous to use a visualiser for innumerable reasons from poor handwriting to a lack of confidence to work real time, via concerns around behaviour and even chewed finger nails. Live modelling can be daunting, but the benefits for our students far outweigh the challenges. There are many ways to do it and do it well. A great mentor when I was training told me: try it three times before you say it doesn't work. Give every single attempt at something new your best effort and chance to succeed and your teaching will improve. There is an approach to live modelling for everyone that is suitable for every group of learners and every classroom.

I have seen live modelling give students the confidence and motivation to have a go. I've seen outcomes improve as I have put a greater emphasis on how to do it. I've seen students feeling successful as they can produce work they are proud of and explain the features of it with the grace of improved expertise. The approach that I have seen creates that elusive and beautiful moment in teaching where you see a student have that 'click' of understanding more than anything else is live modelling.

Essentially, give a person a fish and they will eat for a night, teach them to catch a fish they will eat for the rest of their life.

This book is meant as a practical guide for busy teachers new to live modelling or those who are looking for new approaches to improve their existing practice. Also, school leaders can find approaches and ideas to implement live modelling and improve the impact that teachers can have on the independence of their learners. Each chapter ends with a summary of the key points to remember and an example of live modelling in action.

The book is divided into three parts

Part 1 – Why and how – What is live modelling, what makes it different, special and what do we need to consider in planning and delivering?

Part 2 – Processes Thought narration in working reading and writing live models with strategies for transitioning to independent practice and some concepts around feeding back using the visualiser.

Part 3 – Applications – How to make live modelling inclusive, how to deliver a live modelling agenda as a leader, and the playbook – a collection of practical routines to use in the classroom.

References

Kate Jones (2023). The Curse of Knowledge: A Cognitive Bias all Teachers Should Be Aware of, Evidence Based Education. Accessed 8th September 2024, https://evidencebased. education/the-curse-of-knowledge-a-cognitive-bias-all-teachers-should-be-aware-of/

Mary Kennedy (2016). How Does Professional Development Improve Teaching? *Review of Educational Research.* Accessed 8th September 2024, https://doi.org/10.3102/ 0034654315626800

PART I
Why and how

The practicalities of any pedagogical tool must be scrutinised and considered before any action takes place. Live modelling is at its best when it is a carefully used tool, not a 'quick win'.

This part deals with what we need to think of and do before the bell rings and students arrive.

What and why

Rosenshine's fourth principal of instruction urges teachers to "provide models [because] providing students with models and worked examples can help them learn to solve problems faster".[1] In this, he provides two methods of teaching students: the model and the worked example. I will be defining these as the static model and the live model. So, what are the key differences between these and why should the live model be given pre-eminence?

The static model

Often called a WAGOLL (what a good one looks like), the static model is a completed example that demonstrates some kind of desirable content that a student should identify and replicate. Most often, I have seen them used as an example GCSE script or answer that is analysed with careful questioning. It is prewritten, presented in bulk and selected for a specific element, e.g. a methodical approach to constructing a paragraph, a well-used piece of terminology or a high band or mark against an exam criterion.

The live model

The live model is created in front of the class by the teacher in a step-by-step approach. The same model can be worked for different classes in different ways to adapt to the different needs or abilities of the class. It is bespoke to the class and a skilled live modeller who knows their class can craft the example that the students need, at the pace that they need it with the explanation and layers of scaffolding that allow them to replicate it. Any number of desirable elements can be included in chunks that mitigate cognitive overload. It might be prewritten, but it is presented granularly and organically.

Limitations and benefits

	Limitations	Benefits
Static	Often doesn't account for the students' cognitive loads. Is inert, unresponsive and inflexible to the class and the teacher. Needs careful questioning to unlock its potential as a teaching resource. Requires students to make a sizable jump from seeing to doing.	Easy to set up as a teacher (can be saved or printed to be used year after year) Student exemplar scripts are often easily available from exam boards or can be written quickly.
Live	Requires a level of teacher expertise, purpose and confidence to create a meaningful model. Requires a certain level of technology hardware and proficiency.	Students are more confident and able to replicate steps after seeing them happen. Can be timed and scaled out allowing for adaptation for cognitive load. Is alive in the hands of the teacher and can be whatever their class needs it to be. Allows for the teaching of patterns and routines for behaviour and progress.

For now, I will focus on the static model because the live model elements from this grid will be explored across this book. I am in no way saying that a short and carefully selected WAGOLL doesn't have a place in a teacher's tool kit, nor am I saying that a static model can't be effective, but I do believe that it is much more complicated than printing off a top marks essay to be annotated in class the lesson before an assessment or shoving an example paragraph on a slide next to the success criteria as the students are writing.

Furthermore, it is clear and obvious that what a good one looks like to a top and mid student are different. Here we can see a potential lethal mutation. Some students may only ever see a passing grade standard, compared to a top set student being constantly exposed to top level examples. We can accidentally limit students by inadvertently changing our definition of 'good' to 'good for them'. Building onto this, a three-page grade 7 literature essay is an absolutely terrifying proposition for many students, even those who can go on to achieve that level. An apprentice electrician would never be given the keys to a fully wired-up house and be asked to use it to wire up the house next door from scratch, if anything the process would be so daunting that I would forgive the apprentice for feeling like they can't do it. It's not a lack of resilience if it's an act of self-preservation. In this way, many classroom teachers have a lot to learn from vocational teachers. How many times have you heard that a student who was a real handful in the classroom is doing better at college or on an apprenticeship? I hear examples like this almost every year and it's worth reflecting on this. Vocational activities are often defined by a methodical step-by-step style of instruction. They take complex tasks, like wiring up a house, and reducing them to their simplest, most repeatable form as part of a process; the complex becomes clear and simple. Why can't we do this for writing a 12-mark history exam question?

A poorly selected static model can have a negative impact on a student's self-esteem and motivation (a much underestimated variable when it comes to outcomes). It can even undermine your teaching if you are trying to embed a routine that your exam board exemplar doesn't mirror or if there is a piece of vocabulary that you have not taught yet and becomes a stumbling block. It is also worth remembering that exams are not always conducive to neat handwriting and photocopying can obscure it further. Maybe your top student from last year's exam script is perfect and supports everything you have been teaching, but if the class can't read it, it's pointless. Yes, we could type it up, but does anyone really have time? Why not use their answer as a basis for your live modelled example to save you some preparation?

It is at this point that we need to mention cognitive load. Any kind of problem-solving or extended writing task is immensely challenging to a novice and a WAGOLL can be too much. It's easy for students to get to a point where they can't see the wood for the trees because there are so many things to notice in a full answer. To combat this, the teacher needs to navigate a complex and skilfully constructed series of questioning to check understanding and guide students to notice the desirable elements. I would challenge that it is often easier for all involved to create a live model. Live modelling is more direct for the students and more reliable for the teacher to cover the content they want in the way their class will learn it best.

A static model can be an effective teaching tool, but the effort that needs to go into planning and delivering it to a class is often so specific that even the most devoted professionals can settle on 'that'll do' and instead of helping students to "learn to solve problems faster" the model can muddy the waters then they were not very clear in the first place.

However, live modelling, when done well, can bring clarity and an achievable approach to complex tasks such as completing quadratic equations or writing an essay. Once the process is learned, the knowledge can be applied through it. Live modelling is at its most powerful when it demystifies the thought patterns of the expert and breaks them down into small, manageable and replicable chunks. A WAGOLL presented 'live' will instantly have a greater impact because students can see the steps that go into it. The process of moving through an 'I do' where you demonstrate and narrate, 'we do' where you give the students a voice under close supervision to experiment and practise and 'you do' where students apply what you have presented to them will give a student a clear path to success.

Note

1 Barak Rosenshine, Principles of Instruction Research-Based Strategies That All Teachers Should Know, Teacher Toolkit. Accessed 8th September 2024, https://www.teachertoolkit.co.uk/wp-content/uploads/2018/10/Principles-of-Insruction-Rosenshine.pdf.

2 Planning and preparation

The physical (how)

Any attempt at live modelling must begin with a consideration of the means of sharing the moment with your students. 'Live' means in the room at the very moment and modeling live makes the process you are teaching feel tangible for students to understand. They need to see it and hear it, so you need a way to put it in front of them.

The three most common approaches are a whiteboard, typing live onto a document on a screen or using a visualiser. These all have pros and cons and might be a progression model for those new to the approach or gaining confidence.

	Pros	**Cons**
Visualiser	• Your work can be saved and referred back to on a sheet or a teacher's exercise book. • Adding notes is easy using margins or sticky notes. • It mirrors your students' work for ease of translation. • Mobile, I have a standing desk that I teach from so I can monitor the room. • Flexible, you can use it to view student work for peer assessment or praise.	• Initial expense • Technology reliance. • Your anxiety about your handwriting/fingernails.
Typing onto a document	• Your work can be saved and referred back to or shared via VLEs. • Grids/tables are easy to add.	• You probably need to be sat at your desk. • Technology reliance. • Harder to add notes or labels.

(Continued)

	Pros	**Cons**
Whiteboard	• Probably an existing routine that you can rely on with your students.	• Normally needs to be wiped off regularly. • You have to turn your back to the class. • A lot of classrooms are set up with a screen in the centre spot and TVs are replacing projectors. • Where's my whiteboard pen?

The whiteboard is a staple and often a routine the students are familiar with. It is easy, with the only real challenge being finding a working whiteboard pen and not losing it. However, it is ephemeral in the fact you need to wipe it off and limited in the amount of space if you are going to write it clearly enough for the back of the room to see over the heads of their peers. There are workarounds like taking photos of what you write, but these can be a pain and there are simpler solutions.

The use of typing into a document displayed on the board is arguably as simple and deals with the major flaws of the white board. Work can be saved, emailed to students or printed for absentees. However, I find it lacks the tactile flexibility of adding notes, and activities like mind mapping become a challenge. I am sure that some of you are sitting there thinking that I could do X, Y and Z, but I don't know how or where to find out. Also, it traps you at your desk, certainly not a place I like to teach from.

Additionally, these two methods take away the option to share student work or have students work examples themselves. Many teachers of all experience levels struggle to write clearly or in straight lines on a whiteboard, let alone the students, and a student typing at a staff computer is a safeguarding no-no.

To my mind, the best of the bunch is the visualiser. A document camera that is often mobile, limited only by the length of your USB cable. You do have to be accountable for your handwriting (I am a committed cursive writer and I have to force myself to use block lettering every day), but the sheer flexibility of the tool is outstanding. In fact, this book will assume you have a visualiser to hand from this point onwards. The initial outlay can be a challenge in a time of budget constraint, but the impact of a well-used visualiser is worth it. Additionally, they can be shared across a department if needs must.

A space to work from is another consideration. A messy desk provides a challenge to avoid distractions under the camera and adequate space to have your laptop, visualiser, paper to work from and whatever else there might be there. Also, working from your desk in a seated position can test the behaviour management skills of any practitioner. I have seen teachers use lap trays with legs that fold up to enable them to stand and write. I would suggest giving serious consideration to a small standing desk or lectern. This way you can have a separate space and a full range of vision across your classroom.

My set-up features a small standing desk that wheels out from its place against the wall. A two-metre USB extension cable gives me the ability to move around whilst my laptop stays on my seated desk with all of my clutter. I have a full view of every learner in my classroom to monitor engagement and behaviour, whilst having the space to work.

The pedagogical (why)

All teaching is at its maximum impact when it is planned and careful consideration is given to what is being covered and how it is being communicated. Live modelling might happen in the moment, but there needs to be consideration given to what you are going to live model and how you are going to set it up.

The most important questions must always be 'what do I need my students to know or know how to do and how can I present that information in such a way that it can be rooted in deep learning?' I'm not going to claim live modelling is the only tool you should ever use, but I am going to explore planning a sequence of live modelling and some key considerations you could make before the lesson starts.

First, why are you live modelling? This question seems simple, but needs careful consideration. Is there a process that you are aiming to cement in the minds of your students or a key skill that you want to demonstrate?

Setting clear objectives and desirable elements are the first considerations for live modelling. What exactly is the outcome you expect? Live modelling is about demonstrating an expert approach, so what do you want your students to be able to do? What specific features do you want your students to see and start to do?

For example:
Analyse a source with significant author bias in history.
Solve a quadratic equation.
Use pointillism to create a range of textures.
Write an essay that explores Dicken's use of pathetic fallacy in A Christmas Carol.

Each one of these tasks could be an excellent opportunity to live model with a class and each presents unique challenges to a teacher. However, the issue with this is that they are tasks, not objectives and each of these need closer thought in order to make live modelling effectively. They need direction and specificity and this comes from breaking down the desirable elements of an expert's practice.

Analyse a source with significant author bias in history.
Becomes
Critically consider how a writer's point of view can be identified and used to consider potential bias and its impact using embedded examples and evaluative phrases.

Solve a quadratic equation.

Becomes

Recognise a quadratic equation and be able to apply a system to solve it for any example whilst showing your workings.

Use pointillism to create a range of textures.

Becomes

Know how to hold and use a pen or brush to apply paint in a certain style and create a variety of specific texture effects in a famous style.

Write an essay that explores Dicken's use of pathetic fallacy in A Christmas Carol.

Becomes

Identify the impact of a writer's use of pathetic fallacy and know how to communicate a detailed interpretation using embedded quotations, analysis of techniques using terminology and links to the context of Malthusian thought during the Victorian era.

Clarity of purpose leads to clarity of action. Understanding that what you want the students to do and what you want them to know are different things entirely is key. This is the difference between knowledge and expertise. Knowing what pointillism is and recognising it are one thing, but doing it and understanding how it creates meaning is another. Being able to identify a quadratic equation is one thing, but automatically knowing the steps taken to solve it is another, etc.

What we have identified here is the difference between knowing and doing. I know what a back flip is, but I have no idea how to do one. My students might know what pathetic fallacy is, but not how to use it as a tool to examine a writer's creation of meaning, how to communicate this in an essay or how to use it to craft meaning for themselves. The challenge is to identify something specific. If you try to model too many steps too quickly, the impact is diluted.

Once I am really clear on what the point of my task is, my preparation can move into its next step.

Breaking down the process of meeting the objective into steps is the next stage. Demonstration is inevitably a step-by-step method of teaching and each tiny step that our expert minds take needs to be made clear to our students. It is at the point that I start to construct consistent routines and structures, which I will delve deeper into next chapter.

The step-by-step section of planning is the time to become painfully aware that we are experts and we know what to do, how to do it any why we need to do it that way. In live modelling, we model our thinking as much as our planning and every cog that turns in our minds needs to be noticed and articulated to our students.

It can actually be a fulfilling process of mindfully noticing all of the unconscious processes we are used to. Especially for more experienced practitioners, it is refreshing to take a moment to interrogate our routines that have been honed over the terms and reflect on how and why they work. For newer practitioners, it's a chance to start on the right foot with a few carefully considered routines and structures that work for our students as much as us. For leaders it's a vital step for every department to make to ensure high-quality discipline-specific approaches, and routines are adopted and applied with fidelity.

It is at this point it may be a good idea to take a look at mark schemes, assessment objectives and top band examples of answers where applicable. Every exam board has top-level student answers or you may have some within your department that you can break down to the specific choices that led to that high mark being given. It may be that showing workings at specific points attracts marks and students need to be able to follow a series of defined steps to maximise their marks or they are writing analytically and need scaffold and support to construct a detailed answer.

Here's a worked example for English:

Objective: Identify the impact of a writer's use of pathetic fallacy and know how to communicate a detailed interpretation.

1. A clear understanding of what pathetic fallacy is.

2. Identify pathetic fallacy by selecting an appropriate quote from an extract.

3. Plan an answer by annotating the quote. Using language techniques, exploring the impact on a reader and the contextual importance of the text and socio-historical concerns.

4. Sentence-by-sentence construction of an answer using a system that is transferable.

5. Review paragraph and appraise it.

This example is the core process I follow. There are many intricacies that it doesn't take into account, but if a student is able to follow it, they can write a successful analytical paragraph. It is free from the considerations of student engagement at the moment, but already my plan is to live model steps 3 and 4 because that is where I want to have the specific input over what my students are doing it and how they go about it.

At stage 5, my visualiser will come into play again as we utilise peer feedback and additional routines around reflecting and editing.

Once I've done it, we can do one as a class and then they can attempt with independence. This 'fading' approach of 'I do', 'we do' and 'you do' builds the motivation and self-esteem of the learners in your classroom, provides a wealth of scaffolding and focusses your formative assessment to find specific misconceptions.

As my lesson planning continues, I am able to start to consider the activities and how the students will engage with them.

1. A clear understanding of what pathetic fallacy is.

    ○ Activate prior knowledge of pathetic fallacy by explicit pre-teaching tier 3 vocabulary.

- Starter task – odd one out with pictures of a storm, a sunny day and a snowy scene. Oracy opportunity for exploratory talk.

2. Identify pathetic fallacy by selecting an appropriate quote from an extract.
   - Teacher-led reading of a short extract from Dickens' *Bleak House*.
   - Paired work to identify quotes that include the fog in an extract.
   - Rank quotes by how well they answer the question and include an interesting example of pathetic fallacy.

3. Plan an answer by annotating the quote.
   - Establish why type of questions we should be asking of the text. What is the metaphorical effect of the pathetic fallacy? What meaning is created, what is the impact on the reader and why did Dickens craft it in this way?
   - Annotate using a quote explosion technique. Me, we, you fading approach.
   - Students fill in a grid with examples that feeds forward into the structure for writing.

4. Sentence-by-sentence construction of an answer using a separate and well-drilled routine. Ensuring to question and take student feedback on. Make intentional mistakes and ask students to suggest improvements.
   - Embed a quote with a discourse marker.
   - Link the quote to the question with an analytical verb.
   - Spotlight the use of pathetic fallacy and the metaphorical meaning.
   - Explore the impact on a reader.
   - Explore the writer's intention and broader message.

5. Review paragraph and appraise it to create a success criteria.

6. Class model where I prompt and they create using cold calling.

7. Students use their plans to attempt to follow the writing process using my model to mine sentence starters and vocabulary.

8. Peer assessment based on a clear success criteria.

Now I have a whole lesson with a discreet live modelling section. It is based upon a single objective and I have been able to select a range of appropriate pedagogies for different tasks. What's more the routine's transferability is what truly develops their expertise, as we will discuss next chapter.

Lessons like this become second nature and I would teach this whole lesson from my visualiser with a slide for the odd one out starter and a simple 3 × 5 grid printed on A4 if I could muster the strength to walk to the photocopier, but nothing else. I would create the lesson in front of them step by step, modelling what it should look like in their books in addition to the modelling of the expertise around writing. It may look ad hoc, but in reality the planning is just as complex and detailed as it would have been if a lesson with the same outcome was made into a slideshow.

As an addition to this, I might choose to prewrite the paragraph that I am going to model to take a layer of pressure off myself and free up my working memory for questioning and behaviour management. I would still write the paragraph live, but it would be copying for me and still live for the students, also this gives a potential resource to aid inclusion for students to alleviate the pressure to write.

This can be a solution for anyone who is starting out on their live modelling journey, is live modelling something particularly complex or has students who would benefit from labelling a paragraph instead of copying it down and labelling it (there will be more on inclusion and live modelling in Chapter 9).

My prewritten model for year 7 might look something like this:

> At the start of the extract, Dickens describes the "fog cruelly pinching the toes and fingers" of a poor apprentice. This could suggest that the fog is a force of evil because it is causing suffering and pain to a helpless victim. The use of pathetic fallacy personifies the fog and a cruel tormenter who preys on the most vulnerable members of society. The reader feels sympathy for the boy because he is unable to escape or take shelter from the fog because it is surrounding him and filling the city of London. Dickens could have used the fog to capture his views about London as a corrupt city that allows the poor and weak to suffer in his social commentary novel.

I unapologetically model at a higher level than students would be capable of creating independently and I urge you to do the same. This paragraph is designed to have a series of steps that the students will be able to complete one at a time and begins to expose them to higher-order concepts and academic vocabulary and structures. Over time, students will start to try out the more academic style once they have the basis of how to structure an answer. The novice is reliant on rules, but the proficient are able to play and explore with different forms on their way to expert. When they are ready for this, a simple flick back through their exercise book/folder will reveal a host of examples that they can use at will. The seeds you plant in the Autumn term can be harvested in the Spring or Summer.

3 Building the conditions

No plan survives first contact with the enemy. This quote of contended origin captures one of the key reasons many teachers can be reticent to push in new directions and explore different pedagogies. Obviously, we don't think of students as enemies, but so often their attention, or lack thereof, and motivation can present behaviours that are challenging to us and our teaching. Every teacher has a class or lesson slot over their timetable, or has had one at some point in their career, where something new seems too risky and we stick with what we know because it frees up our working memory to deal with behaviour. It is classes like these that routines that we are familiar with and have deliberately practised can take the load off and become touchstones for our students. Often the conditions must be built before live modelling can be deployed effectively.

The importance of routines

Routines play a vital role in every classroom where learning is the priority, they structure transitions, learning and give a basis for challenging content to be delivered. Specifically, they can help to lessen the cognitive load on students and teachers. Cognitive load[1] is the term given to the maximum capacity of the working memory, and once this is exceeded, additional strains on the working memory are lessened or lost. It is widely focussed upon in regard to teach redevelopment, but a short recap is worth exploring. Moreno and Park assume three strains on the cognitive load that use the mind's capacity for learning. Building routines in the classroom and making active decisions about instruction design can free up additional capacity that can be used for deeper thinking.

Intrinsic load is irreducible and comprises the functions of thinking necessary for all of us. Germane load is deep on-task thinking that links what we are learning in the lesson to what we know already. Extraneous loads are distractions to the working memory that take up thinking capacity.

It all sounds so simple, reduce extraneous loads and increase germane load to ensure learning. However, we know how difficult it is to settle a class of year 7s after a contentious lunchtime football match, or the dreaded wasp in the classroom. Our students' extraneous loads are under constant pressure from the phone in their pocket, their smart watch, let alone the superfluous and brightly coloured wall displays and the teacher coming in on a learning walk or to speak to a student.

This is my case for the importance of routines in the classroom, order and predictability can focus the mind on specific tasks and cognitive sequences. When used in live modelling, routines carry a clear expectation of behaviour and quieten extraneous loads on the working memory. The more capacity, the more opportunity for us to stretch our students' germane capacities and create a lasting change in the long-term memory.

How to build automaticity through routines for live modelling

Practically, I focus my routines on lead-ins and by Christmas every student in my class knows what will happen next. By Easter, I can ask any student to predict what we are about to do based on my non-verbal cues: this is automaticity. By making active decisions in instructional design, we reduce the extraneous thoughts of, "what do I have to do now" and open up the germane potential of our learners to think about the worked example itself.

Consider this thinking guide around the selection, development and establishment of routines to gauge the effectiveness of what you do or develop an approach.

Routine design element 1: few and effective

What are the elements of your practice that you want to be repeatable? How do you want it to look when your students do it? Are there aspects of your curriculum that naturally link together?

In regard to live modelling, we need to give students the opportunities to prepare themselves and focus. At the start of a live modelling journey, a specific type of task that you want to get right can be the basis of what you do.

Routine design element 2: script lead-ins

Once you have pondered these questions, you can begin to establish what your routine will look like. I would recommend scripting and practising these to be precise and easy for you to repeat. My routines do not differ from year 7 to 11, the content and complexity do, but the seed I plant in year 7 can bear fruit throughout a student's school career. If our aim is automaticity, our routines need to be the same every time. A script could be a simple word or phrase, when planning answers in English I have plus plans and six packs, the students know what they are and how they should look. Saying these words triggers actions that reduce wasted time and any extraneous cognitive load.

Start small, use a variant on your preferred attention-gathering routine and explain to students what the expectation is. When I say ... I need you to ..., share your pedagogies with students and explain why you are doing it and they will not just comply, they will want to take part.

Routine design element 3: consider interactivity

How can we bring our students into their own learning? Any levels of interactivity can only break down barriers and quicken uptake. Consider call and response strategies. Which triggers can elicit a response from the class.

Routine design element 4: stick with it and praise the positives

Routines need time to become habits. Praise uptake and look to reward. Any student doing the right thing deserves to feel seen and nothing brings students on board like hearing their peers being celebrated.

The power of attention and motivation

"Attention is the gate keeper of learning"writes Peps Mccrea and he adds that "motivation is a system for allocating attention"[2] in his excellent *Motivated Teaching*. We can only learn that which we attend to and we only attend to what matters to us or feels relevant or important. Teenagers can be fickle and capricious creatures, they can be switched on and engaged one day and absent minded and distracted another. The time of day, year, weather, what lesson they just had, what they are doing after school and their peers all seek to drag their attention away by filling their cognitive load with the extraneous. Students' motivations are all different and challenging too: "I'm going to work with my dad as a plumber, so why do I need to read Shakespeare?", "I'm always going to have my phone's calculator, why do I need maths?", "Why do I need to understand why some centuries dead King lost his throne and what effects it had?" These are all valid, yet exasperating, questions that teachers across the globe face on a daily basis. We all have cliché responses, but if we can make it matter and show students a way that means they can feel successful, maybe we can keep them to ourselves.

Attention: building buy-in and making it matter

Live modelling's beauty is that we start with the same as our students: a blank piece of paper. What I call blank page fever is one of the most common complaints of students and often a significant barrier to learning. The attention required to start is when we are at our most fragile. It is at this point when thoughts of weekend plans, lunch time queues for chips and feelings of inadequacy creep in. How many times has a student expressed to you that they don't know how to start, but if they could just get that first sentence down, they would be fine? Every group of learners is different, but there are some almost universal strategies.

Making it matter is a balancing act of epic proportions. Too small and it's trivial and not worth the effort. Too big and it's intimidating and too hard. If "motivation allocates attention based on the best available investment",[3] we can't afford to get it wrong. For huge numbers of students, GCSE exams are either too far away to worry about or so terrifying that they elicit a fear response. Reward points and consequences work for some but not others. If the carrot isn't worth it or the stick isn't big enough, it doesn't matter.

The context of each class and student must be a priority. I've taught top-set year 11s that hung on every word I said if I mentioned the top band of the mark scheme and I've taught students to whom a positive phone call home would inspire effort beyond what I previously thought them capable of. It is often the concrete that motivates, not the abstract. A GCSE exam a year and a half away is so nebulous that it is meaningless to all but the most self-regulatory learners, but a simple process to complete a task that they didn't think they could do feels real and worth the effort.

The simplest motivation is often: you can do it and I will show you how. The context of success is the most universal element that we can tap into. Start small, a sentence using a keyword learned last lesson that feels achievable and can be tied to something more concrete is the bait on the line of writing an essay. Filling in a planning grid makes the extended writing task seem possible. Working through an example with a clear process makes the equation less daunting. Finally, knowing how to be good and understanding that as a stepping stone to being great helps students buy into a process over a term, year or key stage.

We have to consider the student's self-esteem. Apathy is often a symptom of learners who don't trust themselves and, as we suggested before, self-preservation requires they don't try and risk confirming their fears. An apparently apathetic learner is often a learner to whom failure cannot be an option, so give them a taste of success. Scaffold to where it's simple, but not patronising and then fade it away. It takes time and there will be ups and downs, but a whispered, "You told me you couldn't do that 10 minutes ago/ last lesson/ in September", could be how it becomes meaningful.

Pacing the model

In addition to these macro-concepts of motivation, the micro-elements in the lesson also have an impact. The pace of a model can have an impact upon the attention of a class or a student. Too fast and it becomes unachievable (again), but too slow and it's frustrating and patronising. We have to choose the pace of our modelling based on the needs of the class.

Modelling pace	Benefits	Considerations
Exam pace	• Let them see you sweat, but not too much! • They understand that it is hard, but using the approaches you have taught them it can be done at a high level. • Contextual and relatable • Allows them to see a final product/big picture and learn the value of an approach through its application.	• Not ideal for introducing an approach. • It can lack precision if you are putting yourself under pressure. • Can become unrelatable and feel unobtainable. • What are students expected to do while you are writing? If they are trying to keep up, they are not listening or absorbing, but if they are only listening it can be uninteresting
Fast, but measured	• Allows you to thought narrate clearly for students with more cognitive load available for them to listen and learn. • Motivating in the 'keep up' challenge. • Ideal to practise a well-embedded process.	• Are students simply copying down? • Can students 'keep up' should they? • Do students have enough grasp of what you are trying to show them how to do?
Slow and precise	• Maximum explanation and thought narration time with cognitive load available to learning. • Achievable and ideal for explicit process instruction as it is embedded.	• Are students too expert to find value in this pace? Are they bored? • Are students thinking deeply, are you giving them enough to push their cognitive load without leaving space for the extraneous?

The right pace needs to be linked to the activity and its aim. There is no point in writing an exam pace answer for a class who are unsure how to approach it, similarly there is no point in writing a slow sentence-by-sentence model with a class who know the steps and have brought in already. However, a short exam-pace paragraph which is then analysed sentence by sentence and mined for sentence starters or tips has value, as does a slow model where levels of sophistication or what Alex Quigley refers to as "moves"[4] are being built onto existing practices.

Another micro-concept is the size of the steps we are asking students to take. The curse of the expert is that it is so simple to underestimate the challenge of a task. If a student's cognitive load is all accounted for, then they are going to stumble and attention goes as self-esteem drops. This links back to the ideas raised in the importance of planning and repetition of steps. Once the steps are mastered, they can be experimented with. The great artists, more often than not, had to learn the rules before they started breaking them. Joyce wrote Dubliners before he wrote Ulysses and Van Gogh painted still life and landscapes before Starry Night and Cypresses. You have to be good before you can be great and when students think of their expertise as a process, not an outcome, they will take another step towards being self-regulated experts.

Live modelling helps show your class that everyone needs to find a way to get started. We all have a blank page, I'm in this with you, and I need to pile my attention into getting the ball rolling. For instance, I teach a blanket approach for starting literature essays. They read the question using BUG (Box commands, Underline steers and Grab words to use in your answer – more on this later), write 'Overall', and then reword the question into an opinion (I don't call it a thesis statement, an essay is scary enough without the pressure of having a 'thesis'!). Then they go and plan knowing that they have their starting point ready to go and some of the pressure is off. Should their planning throw up something new, then it can just be crossed out and the same step is repeated. Some students outgrow this, as I can adapt their learning to increased levels of eloquence, but every learner has a relatively sophisticated way into their essay. They are confident that they know how to frame their ideas and believe that they have the tools to succeed.

This anecdote is an example of the power of routines, the one sentence each student writes in their year 11 exam has been modelled with the same script tens of times and the student has reached automaticity. Their motivation has become internal because every time they write it they feel successful. I make sure that they understand they are literacy scholars because that's how they start their essays and any examiner will welcome their opinions and be interested in their explanation. They are making an automatic decision, as a writer, based on their collective knowledge. They have become expert in writing opening sentences to literature essays, not much on its own, but that first sentence brings a second, and a third and before they know it there is an essay, that they wrote.

Building the conditions for live modelling is about building a culture in your classroom, pitching the lesson purposefully and finding ways to master the motivation and attention of your students. Live modelling is going to be cognitively challenging for students and they have to buy in for it to succeed.

Notes

1 Jan Plass, Roxana Morena and Roland Brunken, *Cognitive Load Theory* (New York: Cambridge University Press, 2010), 17.
2 Page 18.
3 Page 20.
4 Alex Quigley, Grammar moves for Academic Writing. Accessed 21st February, 2025, https://alexquigley.co.uk/content/images/wordpress/2022/05/CTWG-Top-10-grammar-moves-poster.pdf

References

Peps Mccrea (2020), *Motivated Teaching*.
Jan Plass, Roxana Morena and Roland Brunken, *Cognitive Load Theory* (New York: Cambridge University Press, 2010), 17.

PART 2
Processes and thought narration

Once we are planned and prepped, it's time to do it. How can we deliver learning sequences that maximise the impact of our expertise?

4 I do
Reading

When the Education Endowment Foundation (EEF) looked at how to improve literacy levels in secondary schools they identified disciplinary literacy as their number one recommendation. In other words, students need to be taught to think, read and write like experts in their subject and understand the differences in approach. These are a marker of a student who excels. Therefore, we are placed at the front of our classroom with the impetus of teaching students, not to do what we do, but to think how we think when we are acting as historians, geographers, sports scientists, etc.

It is important to recognise that there is a change in focus when a student moves from the primary to the secondary phase. So often secondary teachers expect students to have learned to read so now they can read to learn. As Alex Quigley sums it up "successful reading helps determine academic success. Reading proves the master skill of school". To extend this idea further, once a student is a skilled reader, they need to be built up to the point where they have the skills to alter their strategies to read like an expert.

What do experts do when they read?

- Experts read with purpose and often go looking for something specific. E.g. the correct numbers within a diagram to calculate the volume of a prism, a pattern within a graph of a chemical reaction over time or how the writer has created a sense of loathing for a character.

- Experts read with their prior knowledge about their subject activated (because they are being purposeful).

- Experts read looking for features that support, augment or challenge their understanding of a topic. They want proof, evidence or refutation.

- Experts select their reading based on predictions of finding what they need within it.

- Experts read actively using strategies they have honed through practice.
- Experts are aware of when they don't understand what they are reading and seek to clarify and question the material and their knowledge/opinions.
- Experts use their newfound knowledge/information to achieve their purpose.

As teachers, we need to take time to recognise that we are expert readers in our subject, we learned those skills either explicitly in school or by hard graft in university libraries. We also have differing techniques that we use for differing tasks. E.G. Reading a novel for pleasure is very different from reading a novel that I am preparing to teach or a non-fiction source I want to use to teach important context to a poem. It differs when I start to read the poem itself.

This book is all about making our expertise explicit through live modelling. Reading seems to be the logical place to start, because that's where so much learning starts. Whether it is reading a source, graph or exam question, breaking down and comprehending differ between disciplines. We need to take a step back before we take a step forward and reflect.

Making our skills explicit to ourselves

The curse of expertise is that we often do things that we don't realise we are doing because we have reached the point of automaticity. If we are going to teach others, we need to break our choices down, interrogate them and then decide how to deliver them in a lesson, scheme of learning or across a Key Stage curriculum.

We must closely identify the choices, decisions and strategies that we are using and explore the different ways we can break these down into teachable skills.

Take this worked example of an English lesson for GCSE poetry – Ozymandias. Reading tasks:

1. Interpreting an illustration of the poem to predict the story.
2. Reading a nonfiction source to explore background context and activate prior knowledge.
3. Pre Learning important vocabulary to ease understanding – pedestal, despair, antique
4. Reading a poem for meaning.
5. Reading a poem to identify devices.
6. Reading a poem for messages and as a political and historical artefact.

The first element of reading is interpreting an image. I interrogate the image using questions such as: what has happened to the statue and why might it have happened? Who might that statue be of and why was it so large? I see it disappearing into the sand and think about who would see it and how it used to be in all of its glory. I reflect on the emotions that it causes in me and the sadness is curtailed by noticing the unpleasant facial expression of the statue.

This is followed by non-fiction reading. This is an historical, informational text about the temples of Abu Simbel (built by Rameses II AKA Ozymandias). It is presented with images with keywords in bold and subtitles for different paragraphs. We discuss ancient Egypt and often students bring up knowledge from primary school or even films or TV shows they have seen.

This text is being used to frame our understanding of Ozymandias as a monument builder and to begin to consider the man behind the statue. I want to know what he built and why he built it and to try to get an insight into the man Shelley was so keen to mock.

As an expert reader, I have clearly defined this purpose as I selected the text and now I need to identify the strategies I am going to use.

1. I am going to scrutinise the images and infer from them. I am going to do this before I have read the text and again after to apply any knowledge I have gained from the reading.

2. The text is organised into sections, so I am going to review the subtitles to begin to consider where I am most likely to find pertinent information. I know I am not looking for historical or architectural insight, so I start to exclude sections that are unlikely to help me achieve my purpose and predict where my attention should be focussed.

3. As I read, I am going to expect vocabulary linked to Ancient Egypt, so I begin to unpack my prior knowledge. I quickly skim and scan the text and I notice that the word hieroglyphs is emboldened and remember what I know about them when I get to that bit.

4. At this point, I begin to closely read the text. I am a literature specialist, so these historical sources are slightly alien to me. I purposefully track with a highlighter looking for references to Rameses II and the monument. I quickly identify that Abu Simbel is fronted with four statues, 20 metres tall of the man himself seated on a throne and crowned.

5. I pause at this point to consider the fact he decided on four statues and imagine walking in under these statues. I notice the adjectives colossal and towering, which aid me in this. I wonder about the man who wanted everyone to look at him in his grandeur and I can start to understand the man. I notice in one of the images that the statues are damaged and I think about how upsetting this would have been to Ozymandias.

6. I am able to use existing knowledge of the Romantic era's philosophy to understand Shelley's derision at the decision to place one above another and exclude

the freedoms of others. I can think about the sand as a natural force and a teacher to educate readers of the perils of Ozymandias' hubris.

When we take the time to really reflect on the steps involved in reading academically, they mount up, but by breaking them down we can identify the skills we need to teach, practise and the questions we need to ask of students.

Vocabulary

Using my visualiser, I can live model every step of the process, including vocabulary acquisition. Not only can I underline and define, I can begin to embed these words in sentences and use them as often as possible.

This is where it is important, again, to remember the novice nature of the learners in front of us. The 'vocabulary gap' is a distressing phenomenon that has been made worse by the COVID pandemic. The Oxford Language report found that 4/10 pupils have "fallen behind in their vocabulary development to the extent that it impacts on their learning". This means that, in regard to modelling the tier 3 disciplinary vocabulary, we need to be increasingly aware of the tier 2 vocabulary that our students might lack.

This begins by being actively aware in the planning stage and foreseeing the issues. Students can't access as experts until they have achieved an automaticity of the intermediate concepts. How can students understand the distance Shelley creates between the speaker and Ozymandias if they do not have an established understanding of the connotations of the word 'antique'?

Live modelling vocabulary has to be more than just writing the definition next to the word, it must be richer and embed that word within the working vocabulary of the student. The use of the Frayer model (there are many other options) prioritises a clear definition and an understanding of how the word is to be used. E.G. antique can be a noun or an adjective without any changes, so students need to interrogate the sentence to find precise meaning. Also, examples and non-examples deepen the understanding of what and what not to do when trying to use the word.

What's more, now that we have identified this word, modelled and discussed its use, we can make a point of deploying it in our written work and thought narrate with precise shared language.

A strategic approach to vocabulary acquisition could see you using those words in other tasks to build the confidence in using the tier 2 words you have identified. In English, I might plan a creative writing lesson focussed on describing finding a treasured antique or a piece of persuasive writing in which I criticise an opposing point of view using antique as an adjective. In history, I could teach the word uprising and then insist on its correct and regular use by putting it into success criteria or planning schemes of work to focus on different uprisings through KS3 and feed into KS4.

As a leader, it can be powerful to identify the tier 2 and 3 vocabularies you would like your students to use confidently and track backwards through your schemes of work to identify where, when and how students are introduced to a word, when they get to recall it to a point that it is embedded. Such an approach can lessen the cognitive load of students at the pinch points of their courses when the content is at its richest and highest stakes. I went as far as establishing shared definitions across my department to build consensus and consistency for students.

> **Example**
>
> Word – equivication/equivocal/unequivocal
>
> Desired use – In *Macbeth*, the witches speak in equivocations. Their highly equivocal prophecies are interpreted by Macbeth and lead him to make decisions that cause his downfall. However, in *An Inspector Calls* the Inspectorspeaks unequivocally in warning and censure of the Birlings and Gerald.
>
> Shared definition – The use of potentially misleading words to conceal the truth. Un – a prefix that makes a word mean the opposite.
>
> Opportunities to introduce and recall – Year 7 – Malala's clarity of message in *I am Malala* is unequivocal about the power of education. Year 8 – the pigs in *Animal Farm* use equivocation to confuse and control the animals. Year 9 – The Narrator in *Blood Brothers* becomes less equivocal as the play progresses and the message of classism becomes clearer.
>
> Practice – aim to use the vocabulary in my teacher talk, modelling of descriptive and persuasive writing and in success criteria for students.
>
> This careful strategy of modelling vocabulary along a spiral curriculum builds knowledge and precision.

Reading strategically – knowing your purpose

There is a vital difference between reading and academic reading, which students are often unaware of. Reading with any purpose other than entertainment requires a different type of focus and strategy because there is the expectation that the reading will be used to do something. If we haven't paid careful attention and utilised our expert skills as we read, we are on the back foot already. Purposeful reading is strategic reading.

I am sure we have all had heart-sinking moments when we realised that students have had a highlighter and a text and either: (A) they have not highlighted anything or (B) they have highlighted everything as may as well have not bothered. The question I pose is has anyone ever taught them how to use a highlighter to strategically read? Students with this knowledge will find the step to independence much simpler.

What would you do with a highlighter under exam conditions? What would be the criteria to determine if something is worth emphasising and being easy to locate again? It has to start with knowing the purpose. If I'm reading an extract from A Christmas Carol to answer a question about Scrooge, I probably won't be trying to highlight words from other characters that do not have direct bearing on Scrooge's character. If I'm reading the opening of a short story to focus on the structure, I probably won't put any emphasis on highlighting the use of metaphor.

These are incredibly specific and focussed reading tasks that have a simple filtering system – does it illuminate my purpose? Yes or no. However, the nuance of more general reading means we need to sieve through and dance along the line of too much or not enough.

A favourite approach of mine is the five Ws. Highlight any information that tells you _who_ the text is about, any information about _where_ or _when_ an event took place, any actions or the effects reveal _what_ happened and the _why_ explores motivations and effects. With this set of criteria, any student should be able to read anything and capture the gist before going back for more specifics.

Chunking reading is also vital for students at a novice or intermediate level. Experts interrogate and interact with what they are reading, we make links and connections, we notice how things fit or how they don't with our existing knowledge base. I teach my students to break the text up and pause between paragraphs to free up some cognitive load for these expert processes. A note in the margin to summarise the paragraph as a discreet topic and how it links backwards to existing knowledge or forwards to achieve a specific purpose.

Fluency, prosody and pronunciation

Apart from the technical and goal-oriented strategies above, modelling reading for our classes has a broader and more general purpose. Our expertise means we have a level of automaticity and skill as a reader. Our voices can be a powerful tool for comprehension. Any text read at under 100 words per minute will be significantly harder to comprehend. This is why strategies of student-led reading (aloud or independently) or 'popcorn' reading can be problematic. An enthusiastic but slow reader can make it so the whole class grinds to a halt.

Fluency refers specifically to the speed and smoothness of the reading and prosody links to the emotion or emphasis a reader places on words as they read aloud. In subjects like science or sport science, with their Latinate words and phrases, pronunciation must be considered. A misconception of pronunciation can grow and fester if it is not noticed and corrected. Arguably, the best way to avoid this is to read it yourself to the class and make sure they hear, and perhaps chorally chant back, the correct pronunciation. No visualiser or technology is required to read with passion and rapt fascination. Pause to share your opinions, ideas and thought processes. Love what you read and show your students why you do.

Reciprocal reading strategies can be leveraged using a visualiser and faded away. Students could observe and read along with you for the first paragraph, then work in pairs for the next one and then complete the rest of the required reading in chunks and with the support they need.

Selecting and presenting reading to students is a consideration that can be rushed and taken for granted. Initially, you need to consider the reading capability of the students in your class. If you select a text with too demanding vocabulary or one that is too long, then student motivation will plummet. Texts can be edited to remove superfluous vocabulary or shortened artificially to aid students' comprehension. An example here is working with a music teacher on developing reading resources and the biographical reading mentioned that the composer in question was a Trotskiest. It very quickly became apparent that this piece of information would be useful for a student in KS5, but superfluous for the KS3 students he was planning for. By interrogating our resources with a view to predicting challenges, we can avoid a lot of them. Some vocabulary is required and the simple step of providing a glossary and planning a vocabulary acquisition activity into the lesson can prepare students.

Presentationally, considering the needs of students who struggle with reading will help all readers in your classroom. Presenting in a clear, dyslexia friendly font, in an appropriate size with wider line spacing will make the text more readable for all, especially if you have chosen something that is going to have an area of academic challenge, it is simple to reduce the strain on students by making it visually accessible. Additionally, taking time to present the text with line numbers means students can ask for specific guidance easier and track more effectively. The inclusion of images and use of bold or underlining to emphasise key words is yet another small step that will have a positive impact.

Stages of reading

In the lesson, the visualiser allows us to live model an approach to a disciplinary text. Some elements of this are universal in high-quality reading instruction, but others will be of greater focus in some subjects than others.

Pre-reading – setting a purpose, skim, scan and predict

Experts read on purpose with a purpose – They choose and use the texts they spend time on. Establishing a purpose for the text is important to build motivation and channel attention. Setting a path of how the reading sits within the lesson by previewing the use of information can build a criterion for students to know what to look for as they read.

Skimming a text utilises quick eye movements to look for words, not to comprehend. Students can be taught this skill using clear criteria. For example, a history teacher could ask students to quickly search for every name by looking for capital letters and dates by looking for numbers. The visualiser can allow us to model and discuss this process for a paragraph before fading our support away.

Scanning is more about looking for the features that have been made to stand out for us as readers. A science teacher preparing to use a page of a textbook can guide students to review emboldened words and interrogate diagrams and pictures for insights. Projecting the images onto a board or screen can make these discussions more inclusive and level the playing field for students who find reading a challenge.

The purpose of these tasks is to allow us to activate prior knowledge. A well-selected and well-timed piece of reading will connect with what a student already knows and understanding this information before they begin reading will ease this process. A strong strategy to support this is prediction because it requires students to take what they know already and begin to apply it. Prediction tasks could look to focus on how we expect this text to support or challenge what we already know in a humanities subject or what we expect to learn about on this page of the science text book.

During reading – clarifying and questioning

Live modelling is about making the internal thought process of the expert external; this can be done in reading as well as writing.

Reading aloud to your class from a text under the visualiser while they read their own copy may seem like duplication, but it serves a purpose. Show students that you use specific strategies that will help them. Using a ruler to track the reading helps any student who loses their place to find their way back, but it also breaks a stigma around a very helpful approach to reading challenging texts. The modelling of mark making and highlighting is invaluable too. Sharing and showing a highlighter strategy alongside active reading, such as marking margins with ticks for interesting or relevant information and question marks for elements that require clarification or rereading. Mostly, it allows you to break, thought narrate and question at the pinch points of comprehension.

A well-timed retrieval question on a piece of vocabulary or a break to turn and talk about a paragraph will support students to join the dots and fill in any gaps. By considering and planning for misconceptions, we can also ensure we are ready to clarify challenging elements of the reading.

After reading: summarise and synthesise

All classroom reading should be low stakes, but it should never be no stakes. The essential attention for a challenging reading task has to be the knowledge that it will be used for something important.

The end of the reading cycle requires that we demonstrate to our students how new knowledge gained can be incorporated to create opinions and ideas. Whatever form the task may take, the visualiser is a tool to share the process of reflecting and drawing knowledge through into writing.

References

Alex Quigley, *Closing the Reading Gap* (Abingdon, Routledge, 2020), 15.

Alex Quigley and Robbie Coleman, Improving Literacy in Secondary Schools. Accessed 8th September 2024, https://d2tic4wvo1iusb.cloudfront.net/production/eef-guidance-reports/literacy-ks3-ks4/EEF_KS3_KS4_LITERACY_GUIDANCE.pdf?v=1725803331

Avnee Morjaria, The Oxford Language Report 2023–2024: Highlights for Schools. Accessed 8th September 2024, https://fdslive.oup.com/www.oup.com/oxed/wordgap/Oxford_Language_Report_2023-24_Building_Vocabulary_At_School.pdf?region=international

5 I do
Writing

A PE teacher would think nothing of demonstrating the correct foot and hand placement for playing a pull shot in a cricket lesson and a dance teacher would work though every moment of their choreography in front of their class using mirrors, so why would we not make a point of not showing students how to write every type of sentence they will need to replicate?

Writing is, quite often, the elephant in the room of education. It is the primary vehicle through which students are asked to display their understanding in the vast majority of their subjects. Even computer science exams, at time of writing, happen offline with a pen, not a keyboard. We spend so much time teaching content and knowledge, that when it comes to using it, students don't know how to get it out of their minds.

It is further made complex by the different types of writing that a student is expected to do in a day. A narrative in English, followed by showing workings using algebraic characters in maths, to constructing a graph from a table of information in science, after lunch it's time to use specific information to explore cause and effect in history and it all finishes with writing about what you did today in French. This is a dizzying array of tasks that have their own specific requirements, criteria and even languages. If each of these five teachers have taught the knowledge the students need to complete the tasks, but didn't model it, it wouldn't be unreasonable for a student to think that the rules of writing a narrative and evoking emotion and tension are the way every writing task should be completed. I am sure that my colleagues in history wouldn't thank me for students trying to craft original emotive similes in their essay and the science teacher probably doesn't want the student worrying about whether their graph has a happy ending. Every teacher of every discipline needs to have a clear understanding of what great writing looks like *in their specific subject discipline*. Once they know this, they need to live model the specific processes, structures and layout in a strategically step-by-step way.

So, what does great writing look like in your subject? Take a recent assessment from one of your classes and then write a full-mark answer, or go to your exam board website and find a student exemplar that found itself in the top band and interrogate it. What nuanced choices did the writer make that were celebrated by the assessment rubric? What were the structures that acted as the frame to share ideas, information or opinions? What language choices do students who achieve at a high level make?

You can't successfully live model until you have a clear and granular understanding of what it is to be great in your discipline. I would remind you at this point that you must remember the curse of the expert. You can do this at a high level because you have been grafting on your discipline for years, but the student who is arriving in your room has just spent the last hour grafting on something completely different with potentially opposite rules. The clarity of your expertise couldn't be higher stakes.

Here's a sample from English literature:

- Essays start with a brief introduction which should engage actively with the question and express an argument or direction of idea. Anything over two to three sentences have rapidly diminishing returns.

- An introduction shouldn't include quotations, but should be specific in response to the question.

- In body paragraphs, a thesis statement should lead the paragraph. It should focus on an element of the overall argument from the introduction and link clearly to the question.

- There should be two to three short quotations embedded into sentences

- Each quotation should be analysed by exploring the methods chosen by the writer and the effect that choice creates.

- Answers should focus on the writer, not the characters or plot – retelling the story must be avoided at all costs.

- A short (one sentence) conclusion is enough to sum up ideas and the overall argument. Anything longer doesn't gather marks at GCSE.

These are the 'rules' and I encourage you to stop and make your own list. Each of these points needs to be carefully explained and modelled at a sentence-by-sentence level. It needs to be repeated and ingrained to a point of automaticity in our students.

These rules are the skeleton of a piece of writing, the next step is to build it up. Again, we need to find the layers that can be replicated across different tasks and teach these clearly and regularly.

I am stalwart in my belief that students are well served by a clear format and structure in the form of an acronym or pattern that they can deploy for any question. I always caveat this with the idea that these structures are meant to be a set of arm bands, never a set of handcuffs. Some students will naturally outgrow them as their expertise increases, but many students I have taught were very well served by a strict(ish) structure at the start. It doesn't matter what my students are asked to do, they know how to do it because they know the rules for writing an essay in English. This may seem controversial to some who believe ideas should flow naturally and creatively. I would suggest that this is another manifestation of the curse of expertise and doesn't, necessarily, remember the student who has just been writing a piece of description and now needs to write an essay. Our students need us to chunk challenging tasks and give them a road map to success: they need to know how to be good before they can start trying to be great.

Over my career, I have had several systems, some were thrust upon me by the school I was working in, some developed more originally, some I have shamelessly stolen from wonderful colleagues and some have morphed as I moved between exam boards with slightly different requirements. What never changed is my approach to using and teaching these patterns: step-by-step modelling an essay like walking up a staircase that eventually students can walk themselves. Some students find a different way to get to the top, but if they should get stuck, the staircase is always there to guide them.

A staircase, not a slope

What is the best spatial metaphor to describe an extended writing task? A highly skilled essay writer takes you with them on a journey, ideas flow together seamlessly and you consider their ideas and they offer evidence that makes their view seem almost incontrovertible. Surely, considering the act of writing this as a gently weaving slope up to the summit of understanding makes sense. So, let's teach our students how to do that! I've spent a lot of time pondering how to make teenagers write like literary scholars, I've even gone back to my university essays and tried to see how I figured it out over time, i've poured over sample essays from colleagues, the exam board and students and the problem is every great essay has the same skeleton, but builds upon that in different ways. There is no formula to writing a great essay. What there is a great expert that knows what works for them. Trying to teach this would be like following a recipe that said (1) Gather ingredients. (2) Make the cake. (3) Serve. Technically correct, but so broad that it is useless.

The realisation that I have come to is that some writer's essays might appear as a slope, but that is because the staircase that was there has been so worn by use that the steps aren't immediately visible. However, on closer inspection you can see their patterns and the shape of a structured approach hidden just under the surface.

Take your skeleton from earlier and now make it practical and usable. If you have a system that you have to or like to use, take a moment to be hyper aware of how each step fits or can be utilised more purposefully. Here is my example:

Skeleton	Practical considerations	Repeatable steps – highly prescriptive at the novice stage
• Essays start with a brief introduction which should engage actively with the question and express an argument or direction of idea. Anything over two to three sentences have rapidly diminishing returns. • An introduction shouldn't include quotations, but should be specific in response to the question.	Blank page fever is terrifying for students, so they need a clear way in to free up their cognitive load at a point of high anxiety. They need to plan and understand how to use it to structure an argument. They need to foreground the specifics of the question and show understanding of the content. They need to establish an argument by referencing key information without becoming descriptive.	BUG [Box, Underline, Grab] for questions six pack or + plan ABC [Answer, background, context] for introductions
• In body paragraphs, a clear opinion linked to the question should lead the paragraph. It should focus on an element of the overall argument from the introduction and link clearly to the question. • There should be two to three short quotations embedded into sentences • Each quotation should be analysed by exploring the methods chosen by the writer and the effect that choice creates. • Answers should focus on the writer, not the characters or plot – retelling the story must be avoided at all costs.	Students will have a plan to follow and an argument to prove – they need to be confident in getting their ideas down onto the page. They need to be able to self-scaffold eventually, but they can follow a clear step by step, even then. They need to place quotations within well-constructed sentences and keep them short – only quoting the text not copying from it. They need to zoom in on specific writers' choices, use relevant terminology and link to the effects created, not simply feature spot. They need to consider an author as a biased decision-maker who is trying to disrupt and manipulate their readers for some specific purpose or goal. They picked every word and structured every sentence on purpose.	Key point Key quotations Key ideas To unlock a text's meaning in body paragraphs.

Skeleton	Practical considerations	Repeatable steps – highly prescriptive at the novice stage
• A short (one sentence) conclusion is enough to sum up ideas and the overall argument. Anything longer doesn't gather marks at GCSE.	They need to not get hung up on this. They need it to be short and sweet.	Ultimate opinion

These repeatable steps are stripped back to the bare bones. I have had students show me social media videos of people trying to suggest a nine-letter acronym that was confusing and robotic. They brought them to me because they understood why such an approach was ridiculous. They had a grand staircase that they were confident in walking, they knew they could pause and linger, even go back a few steps before continuing again. The person on that video was trying to sell them a rope ladder: no space, no support, no freedom, only flimsy promises.

Having a framework that you trust (even if it is not yours) and your students trust is a vital cornerstone to live modelling writing. Helping students to see that there are different stages and then how an expert sees each one as important will build motivation and buy in before delivering better writing after careful live modelling. Every expert in anything begins with clear step-by-step instructions. Every professional footballer had to be taught where to place their non-kicking foot in relation to the ball and what part of their boot to use and where of the ball to strike at some point. Our students are taking part in the process of learning and becoming expert – the novice must be taken into account and the ground work done before we can reasonably expect any flair.

Each step of the process is clear with defined purpose, but now it needs the criteria or elements to be crystal clear. This is the work you need to do with your students to manage their novice cognitive load. Once they know what their sentence should do, they don't have to think about it as much. We can move them away from: how I say it to: what I want to say and towards: how can I say this clearly with coherence and succinctness.

To continue my worked example:

ABC – Literature essay introductions:

Answer:

Overall, [writer's name] uses [key steer word grabbed from the question] as a vehicle to explore [ideas from the plan]

Background:

A one or two sentence summary of your understanding of the text as pertinent to the question.

Context:

Starting your sentence with the writer's name, give a strong opinion of why they decided to include this character or theme in this particular text at that particular time.

Key paragraphs – Literature body paragraphs:

Key point:

A thesis statement from your plan. A clear idea expressed simply.

Key quotes:

Embed two to three short quotes zooming in on each one to explore writer's choice and effect.

Key idea:

Return to your central argument and why the writer bothered by linking to bigger ideas. Use analytical verbs and the writer/text's name more than characters.

Ultimately conclusions:

A single sentence that begins with the word ultimately and returns to your argument.

We are not limiting our students with a tight and claustrophobic structure. As you can see from the example, the start and the end of the essay are tightly controlled because starting and finishing are the hardest things to do. In between, there is choice and nuance within the bounds of clear expectation and purpose. Every sentence has a goal and that is what I will model. I'm modelling sentence structures within my specific discipline, so much more than essay writing.

Here's what it might look like for a question from Romeo and Juliet such as: how does Shakespeare present Lord Capulet as the leader of the Capulet family? Can you identify each stage of the process?

Overall, Shakespeare uses Lord Capulet's leadership of his family as a vehicle to illuminate the dangers of overly passionate and intense emotional reactions without moderation. Lord Capulet begins the play with violence as he longs to join the brawl and his overactive temper and penchant for violence in the face of disobedience costs him everything. Even in his softer moments as a father, his narcissism and willingness to use his family betray him as a manipulative abuser. Shakespeare's Elizabethan play seeks to champion moderation over passion and Lord Capulet is held up to the audience as a warning of the disastrous effects of extreme passion and focus only on the self.

In class, it would sound something like:

(students would use a ruler to double the width of their margin as I do on my visualiser.)

I'm going to begin my introduction by reviewing my plan. I notice that I am going to focus on Lord Capulet's temper, his anger at being disobeyed, his abusive manipulation and his narcissism. I need to include these big ideas in my paragraph, so I'm going to highlight them in my plan.

My first sentence is going to be 'A' for answer. I'm writing A in my margin and I know I need to remember to start with overall, use words from the question and ideas from my plan. Let's write those in our margin to set our criteria. Time to start writing now, [I write as I say here making sure that I pause to give students time to write and listen. I also narrate my punctuation – it will take longer than you think to write three sentences.] I start with overall comma because an adverbial sentence opener is always in a subordinate clause. Now I'm going to use the writer's name next because the question asks me how Shakespeare presents Lord Capulet, not what Lord Capulet does. Notice how I'm using the question to help me write this sentence as I continue to use the steer phrase. Note as well that I am writing in the present tense because that is expected in English essays. Coming up next is a great phrase that is so helpful and worth remembering: as a vehicle to. This phrase forces you to focus more on the writer than the character. Now I need an analytical verb that captures what Shakespeare was up to. I'm going to pick illuminate here because Lord Capulet is a tool for Shakespeare to spread his message in the play – the danger of passion without moderation. So what does Lord Capulet actually do? He's really passionate and intense in how he reacts to things – let's put that in next and link it to the big idea. Full stop to end the sentence.

Let's check our criteria for this sentence and we've got it all in. Success. When you have a go on your own you can use parts of this sentence to answer any essay in English. Let's highlight the bits you can magpie into your work ….

The thought narration is minute and precise. I'm using the specific vocabulary that I have been focusing on such as steer phrases and analytical verbs to help students create a mental model of writing an A sentence within an ABC introduction, but also link it back to the mental model of how to plan an answer. I want them to understand they are like a conveyor belt that does the same things in the same order to make similar final products. Essay questions come in and essays come out. These essays will likely be cookie cutter to begin with, but the novice needs structures to adhere to and with mastery of the structures comes the expertise to explore and be organic.

An introduction can be modelled fully after planning and discussion with the class. The exercise here is to use a plan and an agreed structure to execute at a high level. A student should be reassured that if they have clear planning strategies and a clear structure that they can answer any essay question they are faced with.

It is worth mentioning that you need to be precise in a lesson about what the actual modelled skill will be. Rome wasn't built in a day and neither is expertise. If the skill you are trying to teach is planning, then don't try and write an introduction in that lesson; the leap is too big. You risk undoing the success and self-esteem you are building if you ask them to use a tool that they are not fully focused on and confident with. The risk of misconceptions becoming embedded is too great if we don't take control and 'drive' the initial introduction and acquisition of each element. Live modelling in this way needs to be seen as a series of lessons over time, not a stand-alone silver bullet. It will take time and repetition because are learners need it to

Consider a learning sequence of introducing students to a system such as ABC introductions:

N.B. I am imagining that the content has been covered and the students have studied and revised Lord Capulet's role in Romeo and Juliet, additionally I would furnish my students with a knowledge organiser because we need the knowledge to have a level of automaticity to reduce the cognitive load based around the skill of essay writing. Specific goals and learning is the core to live modelling well.

1. Planning lesson based around understanding the question and collecting the knowledge. Using a planning system the students already know or embedding and modelling the way you want a piece of writing planned.

2. Introduce the ABC system and break down each sentence to its clear role and practical considerations. Live model an introduction sentence by sentence as you thought narrate the decisions you are making. I would consider having a prewritten model that I would be copying under the visualiser to allude to spontaneous creation. Students would copy the model down (some who need adaptations would be given a typed version) and make prompt notes in a double width margin or double-spaced lines (see the final chapter for how these are used). Students would then be provided with a plan to a similar, but different task (Lord Capulet as a father figure) for them to try. The focus is on them transferring as much from the model as possible and finding moments of repetition (sentence starters, specific analytical verbs or phrases, etc.). Teacher finishes the lesson by show-calling successful examples.

3. Students review their introductions from the previous lessons using self or peer assessment regimes. Specific misconceptions that were noted in the writing last lesson are addressed and retaught before students are given a part completed plan to finish and then an opportunity to independently write an ABC introduction.

Within this cycle are clear lesson foci and a graduated approach to introducing a series of specific, distinct, but linked skills. Planning will always precede introduction writing, but if we want students to plan like experts, we need to spend time teaching them how and the same goes for each and every single sentence. Don't teach them how to write an essay, teach them how to construct great sentences and stack them up and the essay will take care of itself.

Good to great

Imagine we are pursuing the same essay, the introduction is written and we are ready to move onto the next step. Imagine also that students are not complete novices at writing body paragraphs. They have had the double width margin sentence role lesson sequence and are beginning to progress: they have learned to be good, but now it's time to start them on a path to greatness.

This time I am going to ask students to write the initial model double line spaced. We write the following paragraph [at differing levels of collaboration depending on the class and where they sit on the scale of expertise. I might have a prewritten good and great paragraph next to, but not under, the visualiser, or I may be ad hoc in writing my paragraph because I have planned the specific skills I will model]. However, the goal is to write something basic and potentially including errors or misconceptions I have noticed during feedback. I am willing to cede some control over the initial model because the skill I am introducing is enhancing the basic and tackling misconceptions. Clarity over what you are modelling is paramount.

Lord Capulet's anger at being disobeyed reveals he is narcissistic and obsessed with his status above all else. When he shouts at Tybalt "am I the master here or you?" the rhetorical question shows his confusion at being challenged by someone below him in the family and he follows this up with the threat "i'll make you quiet" if Tybalt makes a "mutiny among my guests" suggesting that his main concern is what other people think of the Capulet family and how it's high status can be maintained. When Juliet disobeys him he explains he will "give you to my friend" and tells her to "hang, beg, starve, die in the streets" if she will not do as he commands suggesting that he sees her as little more than an object that belongs to him and can be discarded if it displeases him. Shakespeare attacks lord Capulet's insecurity around his status and the narcissism that it has created in him by exploring how two teenagers cause him to lose control and the audience are confronted with the realisation that without moderation and self-control there can be no real power.

At this point, I would present students with a 'greatness criteria' and ask them to review my paragraph in pairs before suggesting where it is good, but not great. In this example, I would be fishing for: SPaG errors (capital letters), lower-level vocabulary, not every quote receives the same analytical attention and the key idea section lacks specificity. Also, I know I want to teach the use of appositives and tonal quote embedding.

This is where the double spaced lines will be used, asking students to select a different colour pen, I begin proposing and inviting editorial suggestions. The capital letters get fixed, the vocabulary is discussed and upgraded (anger becomes rage, etc.), appositives are introduced and added and quotes are better analysed. Students can now write the great paragraph, which may look something like:

Upgraded vocabulary

Lord Capulet's *rage* at being disobeyed reveals he is narcissistic and obsessed with his

Improved specificity by linking to the central argument

status above all else revealing that he is a potent warning against a life ruled by passion.

Added adverbial opening *Upgraded vocabulary* *Appositive phrase*

Rapidly losing self-control, he berates Tybalt, who is set on attacking Romeo and disrupting

Upgraded vocabulary

Juliet meeting Paris, "am I the master here or you?" The rhetorical question *displays* his confusion at being challenged by someone below him in the family and he follows this up

Silly SPaG error

with the threat "i'll make you quiet" if *T*ybalt makes a "mutiny among my guests" suggesting that his main concern is what other people think of the Capulet family and how it's high

More detailed analysis of writer's methods

status can be maintained. Through the personal pronouns "I" and "my", Shakespeare explores how self-obsession leads to narcissism and the loss of control, which is ironic

Linking adverbial to make the point more coherent

because Capulet seeks control over everything else. *Later in the play* when Juliet disobeys him, he explains he will "give you to my friend" and tells her to "hang, beg, starve, die in the streets" if she will not do as he commands suggesting that he sees her as little more than an

Adding specificity to how this example of Capulet's behaviour proves my point

object that belongs to him and can be discarded if it displeases him. Shakespeare powerfully extols the idea that a life ruled by passion leads to a loss of perspective and implies the idea that a more moderate and stoic approach to life makes it easier to achieve personal goals

Silly SPaG error

and power. Shakespeare attacks Lord Capulet's insecurity around his status and the narcissism that it has created in him by exploring how two teenagers cause him to lose control and the audience are confronted with the realisation that without moderation and self-control there can be no real power.

This approach to writing, editing and reviewing, similarly, to the initial writing, is about giving students a mental framework and scaffold. It reveals the questions an expert asks themselves to ascertain how they can make improvements.

At this point, it is worth mentioning the place of intentional mistakes and non-examples within the live modelling process. When we are seen to make, notice and fix mistakes, we are showing that resilience is needed to be an expert and nobody is the finished article or perfect the first draft.

Consider making the kind of silly errors that your students make. Miss a capital letter, get a spelling wrong or repeat a word in a sentence and ask students to notice and correct. There is huge value in writing half a sentence and then deciding to cross it out and start again because it is waffling, as long as you pause and discuss why the new sentence is better using your shared standard of greatness.

When you build a culture of revising and editing your own work, you will see students produce better writing because they have the toolkit to do it and the confidence to know that it doesn't reflect poorly on them if they make a mistake.

The learning sequence would look something like:

1. Students review a good model with a 'greatness criteria' and improvements are modelled. Key sentence structures and components are explicitly taught (in this case adverbial openings and appositive phrases. Students are presented with another good model and are asked to make constructive suggestions.

2. Students write up their 'great version' using their notes from last lesson. The teacher circulates and discusses choices. Specific students are show-called, misconceptions are identified and promising ideas are highlighted. Students use a plan to write independently from scratch with a focus on being great.

3. Students are presented with a new essay question and are asked to plan and write for most of a lesson. Feedback is given live to address misconceptions and celebrate approach to mastery.

These styles of learning sequences can be repeated across key stages and courses. Our aim is to help students reach an expert level of automaticity and this takes time, perseverance and consistent messaging when practising. Next term we might be covering A Christmas Carol and students would be encouraged to look back in their books to activate their prior knowledge of writing essays in my discipline before we start. I would ask my students to review their targets from the last example of this type of writing that we did. It doesn't matter if it was on a different text, because that's not what I am modelling. I am modelling how to write an English essay and, broadly speaking, that doesn't have to change too much. Any reduction in moving parts within complex machinery makes it less likely to break down or go wrong. Interrogate your expertise to find the elements that sit in the centre of a Venn diagram comparing the different tasks you need students to complete independently for them to excel in your discipline. This is what you need to live model strategically and repetitively over weeks, terms and years.

I defy anyone to say that this is narrowing a student's experience in any subject. A carpenter doesn't have his work narrowed everytime he uses a drill. He uses the drill to make whatever he wants on any number of projects big or small. They use the drill because that is what it is designed for and it makes their lives easier by getting them to their end goal more efficiently. Writing is a tool for showing understanding and like any tool, the use needs to be learned and practised before it can be mastered.

What are the students doing?

There is a challenging balance to be struck when answering this question and this is the skill of teaching. I have taught classes that I knew I was able to live model an entire paragraph in one go and know that they would write it, with attendant notes. I have had classes where I was aware that some students' cognitive load would be filled by copying and lose all value of the live model if I were to write for more than a sentence. I've taught in rooms where the technical facilities or lighting were poor and students at the back would struggle to see the board. This is where knowing your class and adaptive teaching need to be carefully considered.

There are different ways of delivering live modelled work that make them accessible to all. These are discussed in greater detail in a later chapter, but attention and motivation are fickle and can be lost quickly if not considered and students are allowed to be passive.

Here are some approaches to running an I do section of a writing lesson. This is not a pick one and always do it situation, it's horses for courses. Take into account where your students are in regard to their expertise, what specific skill you are focussed upon and what is going to move students towards independence. These three examples have a descending impact on cognitive load and represent some ways you can adapt your live modelling successfully.

If I write it, you write it

It does what it says on the tin, students [and I use the next word with great trepidation because of the connotations it can have if not used well] copy what you write and store it in their book. They are exposed to your careful thought narration and I would always use this in conjunction with a wide margin to capture key notes and ideas.

This is a slow process because you have to move at the pace of the slowest writer and all students run the risk of becoming disengaged if they think the activity is to copy only and don't have the healthy tension of knowing that they will have to do something with it later.

I would be very hesitant to use this process for more than a few sentences at a time or accept that I will take a whole lesson to model a single detailed example. There is a place for lessons like these, but the motivation required for students to remain engaged is enormous.

Self-scaffolding

This is another technique that relies on the double-width margin. Students watch your live model being created, but instead of copying down what you write they focus on your thought narration and what you say. Their aim is to make themselves a step-by-step guide or note down phrases that they can use in their margin before they write their own model next to their notes.

This approach frees up their cognitive load from copying down and focuses them on the most important part: what you are saying as the expert. However, it is easy for them to miss key ideas and phrases unless you specifically point them out or scaffold what you want them to put in the margin. The quality of notes taken by different students is a potential barrier and when you are head down writing, behaviour can slip.

I would always set non-negotiables on what I want in the margin and suggest they also write their own notes in addition to the scaffold you are setting them up with.

Annotate

This approach initially seems like it isn't live modelling at all, but the delivery is key.

Students are given a copy of the example you are about to write. It may be the whole class, or just a couple of students who need adaptations, but they have it all there. I then write the model, copying from one I wrote earlier, *which I do not display under the visualiser*. The goal is for students to annotate parts of my live model from my thought narration. They can highlight or make notes and then have a starting point for their own writing.

All of these approaches take careful embedding as classroom habits and routines. A reminder that creating the conditions is vital to success.

6

We do – you do

Syphoning experience and feeding back

Growing up playing rugby, I often heard the phrase "you have to earn the right to go wide" parroted by coaches. For the uninitiated, 'going wide' means getting the ball to the wingers in space so they can score, but you can't just pass it directly to them because they will get flattened. 'Earning the right' meant doing all the hard, annoying and repetitive grunt work in the middle of the field: carrying hard to draw defenders in, getting up off the ground faster than your opponent and all of the other things that would make your lungs burst. The wisdom in this phrase is that success is built on hard work, specifically by following a process that adapts based on what you see to get you to the outcome you desire. 'We do' is earning the right, it's the battle that is easier to skip, but the desired outcome will be that much harder if the process isn't adhered to. Our students are the wingers, they can score if we get them the ball in space, but space needs to be made, it doesn't just appear, and it's made by hard grunt work.

Without a focus on students using our expertise to improve theirs, we are just showing off. This stage in any live modelling process is challenging because it requires students to draw upon what you have modelled and begin to use it more independently. This chapter will explore strategies for guiding students instead of drawing them along a process to a point where they are free and confident to try for themselves before the next cycle of identifying misconceptions and the modelling process can begin.

It is vital to take pains to gauge students' confidence levels and understanding of the tenets you have chosen and explored. It would be foolhardy to leap from you writing a paragraph to students being expected to match your expert level without allowing them supported and scaffolded practice. Moving through a 'we do' process of collaborative exploration before allowing students to independently begin to embed the skills you have decided they require offers them a chance to make an attempt with a safety net. When we specifically aim to relieve that pressure, we build psychological safety that encourages earnest attempts as they move into the 'you do' stage where they have to prove themselves.

Overall, this part of the live modelling process represents a change in our role. We cease to be the driving force behind the writing, but transition into a guide before leaving them with a roadmap to complete the journey themselves. We have to be prepared for them to stumble and make mistakes. This is an inevitable part of becoming an expert and is actually to be actively encouraged. However, we can't allow misconceptions to go unchecked and unchallenged and that is why the we do section is too important to ignore if the I do section is to be a success.

We do – identifying when we can do

This is a stage of collaboration, which can be challenging to navigate in a room where you are heavily outnumbered and have a host of different points of the scale of expertise.

Between the I do and we do sections there is a necessary break for formative assessment. We need to identify if we have successfully laid the foundations of procedural understanding for all of our students. As is always the case with learning, some students will need additional support or scaffolding – if we ask them to collaborate without clarity they will only get in their own way and limit the progress they can make.

This is not a book on formative assessment and there are so many ways that this can be completed: mini whiteboards, targeted questions, etc. What is important is understanding what you are assessing: do they know the procedure that they are about to attempt to apply?

If you have followed my suggestions from previous chapters, you have identified specific skills or processes that you are modelling. The Goldilocks zone of not too many elements to be overwhelming, but enough to be challenging requires you to accept that students have to be good before they can be great. If you are helping them to understand a step-by-step 'flowchart' type approach then it doesn't matter if their sentence stems are all the same in every paragraph. Once the system is embedded, then it is time to model different ways to construct sentences within your discipline. This is where the 'we do' stage can all come tumbling down. If we have carefully considered where our learners are, what their broadest barrier is and worked on a specific skill set, their cognitive load should have capacity to begin to contribute to that process.

If members of the class are still struggling, then it can be time to try a different approach. We can't do the same thing again and hope that they can get it, but we can chunk the process down and still work collaboratively, but with different burdens.

We do – levels of dependence

If the task you are teaching is challenging enough to require expertise to approach it, then it can't be a surprise that students, even with the scaffold of collaboration, may still require specific and chunked support.

A high dependency 'we do' process can look similar to the 'I do', but holds subtle differences that can 'spell out' the process explicitly. This stage requires clear calling back to the I do model. Begin by reviewing the model you constructed together and breaking it down. Using a highlighter to make the sentences apparent draws into a discussion of role and process that strengthens the schemas students have in how the abstract process becomes concrete.

"Where in the process are we now?"
"What was this sentence's job?"
"How do you know"
"What have I chosen to do to achieve that purpose?
"What part of the sentence could be a sentence starter we can use in the next paragraph?"

These questions are carefully ordered to begin drawing students along the process and reminding them that we are writing sentence by sentence with purpose. Notice how these sentences begin by exploring the concrete example that we have created. Next, the thinking behind that concrete example is broken down and examined minutely. Finally we begin to identify what they need to know and use if they are going to be successful independently.

At this high dependency stage, we can turn the live modelling process into a cloze activity. A writing frame gives students a point to begin with thus reducing their cognitive load. It is, in fact, their ideas that we are trying to help them get onto the page and once they understand how they can do it we can begin to remove the training wheels and allow them more independence. We can't fear repetitive writing at this stage. To do so would be to lose our focus on generating expertise. The novice requires structured practice and repetition in order to gain the level of the expert: repetitive writers will gradually become independent creative writers given the time to embed the basic skills.

If the process that your live modelling is more specific than generic, then consider an ingredient list approach. This reduces some of the overwhelming choices that students have to make and encourages them to look back at the recipe (that 'I do' model) to see how to use them successfully.

"What is the interesting and important part of this sentence?"
"Where else have I done something similar in my example?"
"How could we transfer that part into a sentence about X?"

This example of a string of questions displays a more minute approach to modifying a student's approach to the writing process. It becomes more granular by looking at a sentence as a collection of different elements to achieve a purpose: a precision instrument over a blunt one.

At this high dependency stage of collaboration, Students need success criteria that, whilst requiring them to make their own choices, allow them to focus on the specific and important elements of what we are trying to get them to be able to do. We've spoken in previous chapters about the importance of incredibly specific criteria and foci for the live modelling process and it is this stage that requires us to be clear and focused. The challenging part for us, as experts, is breaking down what we do because we are experts. If we skip down on that process then students will struggle to collaborate with us.

If you find that your students remain stuck at the high dependency stage of 'we do', it is always worthwhile spending time going back to the success criteria, having students write it down in their books and maybe even refining it even further. We can reduce the strain on a student's cognitive load by making it crystal clear precisely what we are trying to get them to do with us. Collaboration at different levels of expertise requires a clarity of purpose and if our criteria are too generic, our students can easily become overwhelmed by the scale of options that they have available.

For example:

Generic criteria:

- Include a 'big idea' that links to the question.
- Consider the writer's purpose.

Specific criteria:

- Begin your sentence with: Overall, [writer's name] …
- Use words from the question
- Use an analytical verb that I used in my model paragraph.
- Include the phrase: As a vehicle to …

A highly dependent student would look at the generic criteria and understandably feel overwhelmed or confused. They might have big ideas identified in their plans, they might have a secure understanding of the writer's purpose, but they might not yet understand how that knowledge links up with their actions as an analytical writer. The more specific criteria gives the structure, it reduces their available choices and Focuses their attention. It also draws them back to the model paragraph that the expert in the room constructed and encourages them to flip backwards and forwards within the lesson to continuously revisit and use the 'I do' model.

Once students display a grasp of the process, they can become much more active collaborators. Our role as a guide here is specifically important; they are not pure novices anymore, but they are certainly not experts yet. There is a balance to be struck between allowing them to experiment and suggest and maintaining the integrity of our model. Right is right, but there is seldom a single right answer.

Students at this lower dependency level can be invited to collaborate through suggestions and dictation to us under the visualiser. A low dependency 'we do' classroom cannot be silent: our focus on oracy and our students practising the stages with our support is paramount. The use of oracy with bouncing and refining will allow students to prepare to attempt the task themselves.

Oracy is so much more than talking, oracy is the ability to think through talk and express challenging ideas around a specific task. Students need to be able to communicate with confidence and clarity with their peers and with you. This requires a level of psychological safety and routine to be embedded into habit in the classroom to work at its peak efficiency. We work off the basic concept that if you can say it, you can write it.

A structured oracy routine of turn and talk enables students a space to experiment when it is done well, but it is so easy for it to come unstuck and unstructured. The challenges of turn and talk are linked totally to motivation and social factors. Where it is easy or preferable for students to have an off topic conversation, they will. We are asking them to complete a cognitively challenging task and if they don't know where to start: they won't. Behaviour management and high expectations must be maintained at this crucial stage in the live modelling process or the processes won't stick as we desire them to.

The ingredients for a successful turn and talk oracy routine are:

- Motivation to meet expectations.
- Clarity of purpose (a good prompt).
- Suitably developed knowledge or information to have something to say.
- Time to listen and respond by building or challenging points.
- Accountable feedback.

Shortcomings in any of these areas can have a detrimental impact on the quality of the 'we do' activity.

Motivation to meet expectations

A student needs to know that they must stay on task and maintain a professional relationship with their talk peers. Seating plans are vital because friends will often lapse into discussing after-school plans or what's on offer in the canteen today, but students without a sense of trust between them can become one-sided lectures or silent dead zones. Also, the struggle of students absent means that a level of flexibility is needed. Ultimately, any deviation from the task is a choice to step away from learning that we cannot and should not tolerate. Introducing the expectations and taking time to build the routine will pay dividends. Enforcement isn't necessary once you have established a culture of oracy. The expectations of discussion, turn taking and focus can be built and supported. Provide sentence starters for oracy tasks to remove the pressure of starting, reward and celebrate students engaging and practise your most confused expression for anyone not taking part fully.

Clarity of purpose

Students need to know what they are doing and why they are doing it. Posing a high quality prompt or question is necessary for students to develop ideas; turn and talk is a discussion space. If you are collecting a basic comprehension or procedural point, a basic targeted question will always be more effective, a targeted question identifies the gaps, but turn and talk starts to fill them. This need not be a complicated question, but it deserves to be considered. It must draw on the specific skill being modelled and act as a bridge between the 'I do' model and the 'you do' without becoming multifaceted and confusing.

Suitably developed knowledge or information to have something to say

Students must be ready for this step up in rigour. Up to this point, you have been driving them or leading them by the hand and this could very well be their first attempt. Rushing to this step without correctly assessing a class's readiness for it will breed vagueness and confusion. This can manifest itself in the form of misconceptions, which could threaten the long-term goal of mastery.

Time to listen and respond by building or challenging points

This stage can't be rushed, but it can't be drawn out either. This is the students' first true 'hands on' experience and they need time and space to explore their ideas without running out of things to say. Your monitoring of uptake and student contributions must guide you to give this task more or less time than you originally considered.

Accountable feedback

Linking to the first item on this list, students must feedback their discussion's findings or ideas. This accountability needs to be clear from the start and build up over time to a habitual point. However, the term accountability here doesn't only link to behavioural considerations. It also links to their ideas and the willingness to explain or even defend them.

Collecting student responses, bouncing and refining

Feedback of student responses can be collected in different ways based on your group and your task. During these times, there is an opportunity to bounce challenges and questions with the aim of refining the quality of student thinking, talking and, therefore, writing. The role of the teacher in this phase is as a guide, not a director, so consider how to empower them to draw your 'I do' model through into their own work.

The opportunities to bounce student suggestions around the room provide options for refining on the most granular level. The collaborative editing and improvement gives you more opportunities to explicitly display expert thought processes and provide reminders to the class. Basically, it is in this step that you have the opportunity to 'punch' home the key messages to students in the last stage before independence.

The method of delivery can give different opportunities for students to focus on different elements by emphasising parts of the process. Additionally, different classes will work better with different approaches.

Dictation

A student or students dictate what they think you should write leaving opportunities for you to question their thinking and deepen their thinking. Students can add, annotate or improve their own examples or write down the 'we do' as a class model. This allows the messages of the 'I do' to be reinforced clearly and allows you to exert more control over the crafting stages.

Students as editors

In this approach, you begin to model at a basic level and students are given a prompt, maybe a single knock, as a means to interrupt you and make editorial suggestions. This requires clear criteria or more developed expertise from students, not to mention confidence. Some students love the opportunity to correct the teacher and others find it a challenge, so like to knock a bit too much: pick your battles.

Bounce and improve

This approach to the 'we do' places the impetus on sentence by sentence or even word by word level crafting. Using targeted questioning, we can draw out a dictation before bouncing editorial suggestions or improvements. Potentially, you could collect three to four examples from student discussions before leading the class to combine them for the best possible example. Alternatively, there can be wonderful opportunities asking students to select specific words or phrases to use and working out how they can be interwoven.

Attempting independence: you do

The foundations have been laid, the path is clear and well mapped, they have been led part of the way, guided in some and now they need to carry on their journey independently.

Students need opportunities to practise and prove they can draw on the reservoir of expertise that you have been filling. They need to draw your expertise through their own work: they need to do it themselves. As we mentioned at the start of this book, the vast majority of students end their tutelage with you in a strange and silent examination room with nothing but their pens and their wits about them. The final stage in the process is to let them try, and inevitably stumble, in the safe environment of your classroom, where you are there to pick them up. If you have timed and designed the learning sequence correctly using effective formative assessment techniques to identify initial misconceptions, students should be ready to try.

It is really important to remember that we are not asking them to 'prove' that they can do a skill in isolation. We are asking them to use an expert approach to a very specific problem. We are showing them what an expert does when that problem comes up and giving them the knowledge they need to identify and solve the challenge.

Using criteria to join the dots

Begin 'you do' sections with a recapping of the key criteria to direct student attention and manage cognitive load at this pinch point. Often, students need to be reminded of the processes and goals. These should be specific and everything extraneous should be mitigated with scaffolding that provides a framework to apply the new learning to. Remember our previous points that modelling essay writing is far too challenging and gargantuan of a task and many students will lose motivation. If your lesson is on modelling sentences that use fronted adverbials to embed a quote, give them the quote! I've been guilty of this myself when I lose specificity at the moment when students need it most.

Redrawing students' attention back to the criteria allows you to highlight where you have used it in the 'I do' and 'we do' sanctions of the lesson, it allows you to remind students of the process that they are taking the next step on and frame it in a way that seems manageable. It is the ultimate activating of prior knowledge.

It also sets the expectations of what we want them to do and this is where it can be too easy to get carried away. If you haven't been doing a lesson on writing whole paragraphs, the only reason students should be writing whole paragraphs is because you are in a part of a wider learning sequence where the previous parts of that paragraph have been worked on. Even then, it has the potential to dilute the impact. It could be that the 'you do' is further separated into specific practice and in context practice. The end goal is the flexibility to use specific skills on purpose in a responsive manner, but that end goal might be a long way off. Consolidate the learning of the lesson and if the lesson is well planned, executed and timed the end goal will become a reality.

I often begin the 'you do' section of the lesson by returning to my model and physically highlighting parts of my answer that they can either steal entirely or use as a foundation for their own work. In this lesson, that part of the sentence is just window dressing, it's not the goal of the process, so I have to be happy to accept a high level of magpieing because I want my students' focus to be on the part of the process that matters today. Draw attention to the decisions that were made in the 'I and we do' sections that made success happen and set them the challenge of repeating that success.

Timing is important here, the temptation to squeeze in a 'you do' in the last five minutes of a lesson will always be there, but it is often not the time or place for the culmination of a lot of powerful learning. A 'you do' can reasonably be a single sentence, a paragraph or a whole essay. It might be the same sentence starter five times with different information. Using a timer to create some healthy tension is a powerful tool, but sometimes five minutes will do more than 15 in the development of expertise.

The 'you do' is not a plenary task, it's a vital part of the lesson sequence, but it is not an opportunity to gauge the learning of the whole class. Treating it this way puts the focus on the piece of writing as the learning, where actually it is the approach and skill set that we are trying to teach. When the piece of writing, not the approach to writing, is seen as the goal, students should be forgiven for not understanding the nuanced links between tasks. Extended writing can be an exceptional way to see if students have understood knowledge or information in a way that they are able to communicate it back in a different form, but in a live modelling sequence it dilutes the key messages of how to approach writing in a way that can be transferred across different tasks within a discipline.

Monitoring for misconceptions: moving backwards to go forwards

As your students write, you gain an opportunity to live mark and monitor for misconceptions. It is vital that this is actively centred around the chosen and modelled skills, key knowledge and quality and accuracy of communication primarily. If we begin to move the goalposts as students are writing, we increase the pressure on their cognitive load.

Some things we should be willing to let slide and some thighs we shouldn't. Consider Mr Watson's year 8 history lesson where students are working on the skill of comparing the impact of different causes of a historical event using comparative connectives. Students have been taught the knowledge before the live modelling sequence began and have been supported in that knowledge during it, but misconceptions around this knowledge may still arise and need to be identified and fixed. This is the tension between the micro and the macro. Students are being taught a skill that will very clearly translate across their time in KS3, 4 and beyond, but knowledge that is important for the current unit, but may not have the broader impact on their final outcomes. This doesn't make it unimportant, rather its importance is different! Additionally, students must write well with accuracy because it is a life skill and has the broadest impact outside of reading skills on a student's outcomes, in my opinion.

Mr Watson begins his circulation to live mark, sees three students and reads over their shoulders.

Ra'marn has misused a qualifying connective to compare the impacts of two events and is detracting from his overall argument. This is a disciplinary misconception and Mr Watson can stop Ra'marn, underline the offending connective and use targeted questions to help Ra'marn see that what he wrote as his argument is not being carried through his answer and it is losing coherency as a historical essay. He focuses on the 'I do' and 'we do' sections of the lesson and Ra'marn can articulate the change he wants to make and then edits his work.

Casey has used connectives well, but has missed commas and has a habit of capitalising every 'P' in his work. Mr Watson circles the capitalisation mistakes and draws Casey's attention to how commas were used in the 'I do' section of the lesson while explaining the rule of commas before connectives mid-sentence, but after connectives at the start of a sentence. Casey is guided to add the commas into his work.

Sharna used connectives well and her writing is grammatically correct, but she has recalled a piece of information from year 7 about WWI and is incorrectly using it to discuss WWII. Mr Watson points this out and directs Sharna to her knowledge organiser. He tells her to use the same sentence structure from the 'I do', but edit it to contain a different piece of information that they select together.

In each of these moments, Mr Watson may choose to alter his volume in his feedback. When he is talking to Ra'marn and Casey, he sometimes speaks at normal volume to highlight to the whole class to check their introduction and connective uses are coherent and to reiterate the comma rule. For Sharna, he speaks in a whisper for her to manage her self-esteem and motivation.

All three of these misconceptions have been identified and challenged. Each of them may trigger Mr Watson to alter his lesson responsively or impact his planning of future lessons, but here they illustrate how the teacher was able to use the 'I do' and 'we do' to scaffold the 'you do'. The previous steps in the process become powerful artefacts that give support and life to the independent task.

Supporting students: rejoining the dots

In the previous example, Sharna had made a micro-mistake which could have been caused by any number of factors from missing lessons causing gaps in knowledge to a slip in concentration. Casey has made a general macro-mistake that Mr Watson identified and challenged. If Casey is lucky enough to be taught by a group of teachers who are all doing this regularly, he is being well supported. However, Ra'marn's error was a disciplinary macro-misconception that Mr Watson needs to immediately take ownership of.

Let's continue the lesson with Mr Watson circulating and imagine that he finds more students around the room who have a breakdown in coherency due to misconceptions around their understanding of the live modelling focus. This is the cue that the class may not be ready for the independence of the 'you do' and Mr Watson needs to track back.

Returning to the 'we do' or even the 'I do' phase is vitally important, but can be difficult to do. There is an inevitable twinge that you haven't taught it well enough, but this is not the case! The students haven't learnt it well enough yet and that is the nature of teaching and an almost inevitable part of novices becoming more expert.

The profundity of the misconception denotes the extent to which the reteaching needs to be done, however often these misconceptions can be dealt with by bringing the class or a part of the class back to a really focussed 'we do'. If your class can manage it, allow those who are confident or you have identified as not having the misconception to continue their 'I do' practice and work with a small group. The benefit of this is now that the process is refined by the very specific knowledge of the very specific misconception. There is an opportunity to use a student's book to help the class see what the misconception is and then work together to find a solution, before they identify if they made the same error and review their work with corrections.

Moving back down the ladder of independence is an important part of live modelling and it only happens when teachers monitor effectively and circulate in the 'you do' phase. It is not a reflection on the quality of your instruction that a student doesn't understand something, it is a symptom of the process of gaining expertise and learning. It takes guts to stop a lesson and go back, but it is a hallmark of truly great teaching.

Changing the timeline: using live marking as formative assessment

So far, we have been focussed on the linear progression through the live modelling cycle, but there are interesting and creative opportunities to alter the sequence and develop skilful writers.

'You do, I do, we do'

By foregrounding independent writing, students get the opportunity to test their knowledge and skills and the teacher has the opportunity to identify misconceptions to focus on with the class. This is a useful approach for a class who have secure knowledge of what they are writing about and an emerging knowledge of the approach or vice versa. Teachers can leverage the writing to look at knowledge or skills when deployed in this order and then can reteach as necessary through 'I do' modelling. Students can then reflect on their own work with a partner or group to make improvements based on your expert model. This is also beneficial for building a culture of reflection and improving in your class because they understand their first 'you do' was not the finished article, but a step on the path of becoming better.

'We do, I do, you do'

This variation can be powerful in exam preparation and practice sessions amongst many other things because it contains the potential for increasing pace. The 'we do' is often slow by the nature of collaboration and allows key messages to be shared as an initial piece is constructed. The 'I do' section is about seeing the criteria being used and students seeing you being willing to use the sentence stems they helped to create can be a powerful motivating factor for them to kick on and extend the answer themselves.

'We do, you do'

By cutting out the 'I do', you empower students who are not complete novices and get them to independent practice faster. This is an approach that is better suited to practising instead of learning a process.

Repeated cycles or sections – 'stripey writing'

Stripey writing is the process of ping ponging between sections of the modelling process and is excellent for layering and building in different elements of the modelled skill. This process adds another ground of 'I do' or 'we do' after the initial 'you do' before students get another chance to practise. At the end of the lesson, the students' books should appear stripey with sections written in black, followed by a section in the colours students use to self-assess flipping backwards and forwards.

A prime example of this is using different connectives to extend sentences. Take Hochman's approach of "because, but, so" for sentence expansion. Two basic sentences are written. The teacher models sentence A using because, students practise using because. Teacher models sentence A using but, students practise, etc.

The repetition of cycles can build layers of complexity and break down tasks or show the different ways an expert can approach a problem. It can also be used to make micro-corrections around address misconceptions.

Show-calling: leveraging peer and self-assessment

Following the 'you do' you have a remarkable opportunity to seize. Your students have completed a task and would be been very mindful in that creation, they should have clearly syphoned your expertise to shape their own. In short, they should be very aware of the choices they made on a word-by-word or sentence-by-sentence level.

During circulation, I identify students who have excelled in a specific element of the process or who need a nudge into greatness. After the task, I show these students' work under the visualiser and models for the class. The feedback can take different forms:

1. Live marking – in this approach I narrate the student's work as I read aloud and identify specific choices on phrasing, word choice or structure. I praise the

elements of the criteria that have been met and I can begin to offer suggestions on how to improve. If this piece of work represents larger sections of the class, they can more easily translate my verbal feedback onto their own writing.

2. Self-assessment – students read their work to the class and narrate or answer questions on the choices they made.

3. Peer assessment – students offer feedback on the work under the visualiser and can be used to articulate the choices of the expert. They may offer examples from their own work or notice a step or choice they missed.

Feedback

In addition to the formative feedback given in class, summative feedback is a vital step in securing student progress through dedicated independent reflection time or any of the host of other feedback systems. This feedback is another opportunity for the visualiser to show its great worth.

The value comes from helping students to link the feedback and practice. It can be very challenging for students to see the connections between the comments or instructions and the piece of work they completed until we show them specifically what we, as experts, mean and how they can begin to emulate us.

A whole class feedback system after an assessment or identified piece of work makes patterned misconceptions clear and allows us to plan on a more individual level for key errors. The limitation of the live modelling approach is that it is not always suitable to individual feedback in a whole class setting, but separating students into small groups to work on a particular element, as the rest of the class complete other tasks, is a valid and effective way to address this.

Whole class feedback is another opportunity to embed the clear criteria you have set, only this time you are armed with the data of knowing what the errors are. Instead of predicting the misconceptions, we are planning to solve them. The embedded routine of 'I do', 'we do' and 'you do' or one of the variations mentioned above can be used as a precision instrument to supercharge your instruction.

My favourite option is to work on a parallel task, one that is working with the same skills, but with slightly different knowledge, in the 'I do' and 'we do'. The nature of feedback on summative tasks is there is a space in time between completion and feedback, so the reactivation of knowledge before we start can be planned for.

Working on the idea that an essay on one character from the class novel was the assessment task, a similar character and question can be used. I would issue students with a completed plan, review the content for knowledge and planning skills and work through a paragraph using the key messages and criteria from the task.

The 'you do' could be to select a paragraph from their work and improve it with a specific focus on implementing the specific focus you have given before students extend their work in full independence.

Putting it all together: when it is time for them to climb the mountain alone

I've put a lot of stock in the fact that we are preparing students for true independence as we build towards a terminal assessment in the book so far, so it is important to remember that students do need to practise the whole process at some point before they are sat in the exam hall.

This is the culmination of everything that you have been teaching them to do and is the moment where you have done everything in your power to manage their cognitive load by embedding processes, approaches and even key phrases or sentence starters for them to use. It is vital that we identify time for them to practise independently, albeit under your watchful gaze, to catch any misconceptions that remain and help them to see how it all fits together. The formative information that you can gather in these lessons will aid your planning of which skills you need to return to and which have been mastered.

Reference

Judith Hochman and Natalie Wexler, *The Writing Revolution* (San Francisco: Jossey-Bass, 2017), 40.

PART 3
Applications

Embedding live modelling within our practice requires considerations beyond the process if it is going to be successful.

Inclusive live modelling
Expertise for all

An inclusive classroom is one where the teacher knows their pupils' needs and makes adaptations to ensure that every student is challenged appropriately and has the support that they need to access every piece of work. We should always teach to the top and support everyone to reach there. However, this is a genuine challenge, especially if you are teaching mixed-ability classes. The juggling act of inclusion can be difficult to do well and very easy to do badly. This chapter includes some strategies that can ensure every student in your class has equal access to your expertise in a way that they can become confident and independent writers.

In my experience, live modelling is a very inclusive way of teaching when inclusion is actively considered and students with additional needs respond really well to the step-by-step practicality of teaching writing. I have found that many students with autistic spectrum conditions, for example, have found real confidence in demystifying the process of writing and making the 'rules' and expectations clear. However, adjustments need to be made in any effective teaching environment and it comes with knowing the needs of the learners in front of you. This chapter will focus on Autistic Spectrum conditions (ASC), moderate learning difficulties (MLD) and dyslexia (an example of a specific learning difficulty SpLD) because these are commonly encountered in a mainstream classroom. There will be a lot of 'may' and 'might' because no two students with these difficulties will be the same.

We can't adapt to what we don't know and seeking out the information about our learners is fundamental to succeeding in the classroom. Whatever system your school has in place for sharing the SEN register and personalised plans, it is paramount that you review and explore these regularly. I have never understood how teachers can go even half a term without going to speak to the SEN team about their classes. Up-to-date information is vital, and the SEN teams of every school I have worked at have been fonts of knowledge and keen to share. Also, they have been really interested in my feedback too, and the conversations have always been valuable two-way dialogues that end up in the student being much more likely to get what they need. No two students with dyslexia will have exactly the same challenges and may display very differently. The fact that defining dyslexia is such a challenge in itself reveals the melting pot of different categories that it encompasses.

Cognitive load – its most profound importance

A student with MLD "will learn at a slower pace and have greater difficulty than their peers in all academic aspects of the curriculum" and therefore will have significant additional demands on their cognitive load. A student with dyslexia might find it difficult to copy from the visualiser projection and their capacity will be so taken up decoding and writing down accurately, that they have to become more focussed on task completion than meaningful learning. An aphorism I have always enjoyed is that students with MLD or SpLD need everything that other students do, but moreso. I have often found that students don't actually want, or need, all singing, all dancing tools, approaches or actions, they just need closer, more chunked guidance with extra practice. It is a balancing act to maintain the motivation of a student without making them feel like they are doing the same exercise over and over again in a subject that they may have quite entrenched negative self-beliefs in, to support them without them feeling crowded, patronised or different and to help them taste success and believe they can do it. This is why knowing them and their specific difficulties is so vital. At the end of the day, the teaching tactics that benefit students with SEN will benefit all students in some way.

For students with additional needs, it is even more crucial that we are consistent, clear and specific with the processes we are teaching. The steps in previous chapters of define the disciplinary process and structure clearly and powerfully sticking to it in a variety of different task concepts is the best place to start. Many students with additional needs will take more repetitions to move into true independence, so providing a consistent framework will support them to gain the desired skill set. In my experience, students with ASC find the clear, step-by-step approach to be beneficial. There is an organisation to their thinking that can be replicated when they can see the relational pathway from one element to another. When a department has a clear vision and a consistent message, the consensus builds capacity for the staff and the students. Every new-year recaps and revisits the processes allowing for them to be embedded and practised with confidence. Variations on what they consider concrete are often challenging for students with additional needs because it expands the demand on their cognitive load.

The tension here comes from the fact other students in the class may need the variations for them to be adequately challenged. Once again, this adds emphasis to the need to develop an effective and high-level disciplinary process for writing. If students are taught something very good and that is the base expectation, we can provide scaffolding for them to access the task. Variations of something very good make it great and provide opportunities for students to seek challenges from a very firm foundational skill set when they are ready. We have high academic expectations as our standard, but we also have a road map as to how that can be developed. Once this is shared and implemented effectively across a whole team, all students will be challenged. We do what we do for all students, but moreso.

Additionally, adaptations such as consistent visual prompts in the form of icons can act as prompts for students to work independently or encourage them to use their exercise books to aid their work; this building of resilience through metacognitive strategies will support all learners. Task trackers are excellent resources for students to access the chunked tasks and not be reliant on remembering a series of instructions, which are, more often than not, verbal and challenging for some people with dyslexia. I would recommend finding or producing a template that records the steps and criteria for each individual part of the task, laminate it and then write on it with a board pen, or encourage students to scaffold their own writing with notes. This can be prewritten or created 'live' by yourself or an LSA (if you are lucky enough to have one with you). This approach spreads the impact of your live modelling by holding the moment in stasis for learners to dip into as they need it. When students know this scaffold is present, their anxiety levels reduce, and a sense of psychological safety is established. Furthermore, a sense of belonging comes from identifying that the teacher is mindfully thinking of them and helping them to succeed.

A combination of this and the double width margin concept from the 'I do' chapter is to create a margin banner with sentence topics and direction. This can be planned alongside the lesson or be centrally planned where a strong departmental approach is embedded. The messages are permanent and glued into their books to be referred back to. This is a process of chunking that captures all that is good in live modelling and supplements effective thought narration by making the links visible and long lasting.

The use of sentence starters, vocabulary and phrase banks are powerful tools that can be planned for and deployed to reduce cognitive load and ease the transition to independence. Mindfully prewriting the model to use set sentence starters means that it can be consistently pulled through the 'we do' into the 'you do'. Alternatively, giving a base set of sentence starters to students who need them and using them as the skeleton of a piece of writing allows you to direct how and where you are adapting them. Students can use the basic set or can begin to include some or all of the adaptations you present if they are ready to move on with them.

Vocabulary and phrase banks give direction and can act as a transition between a cloze activity and independence with a strong set of sentence starters. Generic sentence starters and vocabulary ensures students will need to mindfully complete their sentences to be correct while still having to think in a clear disciplinary manner.

In the chapter on planning and preparing, we mentioned prewriting the model that you are going to produce in the classroom as a means to manage your cognitive load, but this important stage will also allow you to support learners with

SEN. The pressure to 'keep up' is removed because the requirement of capturing the model and the expert approach do not have to happen simultaneously. A double line spaced printed copy with a wide left hand margin can be surreptitiously dropped on a desk or slipped into a book and support that student to access the expertise without the negative impact of feeling different.

However, the most powerful stage of the live modelling process for learners with SEN is often the 'we do' and taking extra time and rigour at this stage is a key strategy for working with learners with SEN.

The 'we do' section of the live modelling process provides the students with a chance to blend their attempts with guidance and scaffolding from the teacher and peers. It is the lowest threat section of the process and a time to organise and refine their thinking into a clear sequence. Any extra time that we can give for students to do this means extra time for uptake and confidence to grow.

Referring to the previous chapter, students with SEN need the 'we do' section of the lesson to move through the process of high dependency to low dependency more sequentially. Instead of making a decision to use a high- or low-dependency approach, students will be better served by having the support of a high-dependency activity followed by the practice of a low-dependency strategy before an option for independent practice is presented.

These extra steps provide the uptake time and give you more influence over students' thinking and choices. It gives you opportunities to catch misconceptions and address them clearly by the fact you are still actively working from the visualiser. You get the extra opportunities students with SEN may need to remove misconceptions.

Closely linked to this idea is the repetition of steps as 'overlearning' the process. The concept of overlearning was introduced to me by the excellent Suffolk Dyslexia Specialist Teaching Team and has become a consistent part of my practice. Quite simply, it is the inclusion of additional repetitions, additional activation of prior knowledge and additional explanations. Students receive the consistent messages 'over' what they may need. This is actually the core of the messages in this whole book, over communicating the processes that students need to be able to complete independently. It is no surprise that a live modelling-focussed classroom can be one where students with SEN flourish. The demystification brings clarity and a set of steps and the repetition allows for it to be embedded and practised. What benefits students with SEN will benefit all students.

Broadly speaking, adaptations can be broken down into: scaffolding, using targeted resources to support students by lowering the strain on their cognitive load; chunking, breaking the task down and offering more time for collective practice and approach, offering more time at the 'we do' stage. Students with SEN need to be carefully considered by all teachers at all times, but the approach of effective live modelling can offer a pre-chunked set of tasks to close any gaps and give the opportunities to succeed to all.

Reference

Recording SEN and Medical Categories Guidance for Schools: January 2019. Accessed 9th September 2024, https://www.education-ni.gov.uk/sites/default/files/publications/education/SEN%20and%20Medical%20Categories%20Guidance%20-%20January%202019_4.pdf

Leading live modelling
A thinking and implementation guide

Implementing any new initiative on a whole school level is a very challenging task and requires careful planning and monitoring for it to be successful. If you are reading this chapter, then you may be about to begin or already on a journey to make the lessons in your school more 'live' and build a culture of live modelling writing across different departments. Live modelling with a visualiser is mainly a writing-based intervention, but it has many other uses in regard to reading and demonstration, and can be a focus in and of itself or a part of a wider approach to improving whole school writing. Previous chapters have focussed on the decisions in lessons by an individual teacher, but the decision-making behind a cultural shift across an organisation needs to be carefully considered. The advice leans on the EEF's school guide to implementation to challenge the thinking behind implementing live modelling and engaging in the practicalities, monitoring and evaluation. The EEF identify the good practice of explore, prepare, deliver and sustain as a powerful, flexible framework to structure the process.

The chapter is laid out as a thinking guide with prompts that are designed to prompt you to consider and prepare well at different stages of the implementation process. The barriers at each stage must be cleared before that stage begins, because a whole school improvement initiative is a very hard thing to pause once it is going.

Explore – finding your why

Why live modelling, why now, why will it improve the experience and diet of the students?

All of these questions require clear and concise thinking before anything can be pitched, yet alone implemented. Live modelling builds expertise, the place where knowledge and skills meet and demystifies the process of writing in a particular discipline and can be very powerful if it is done right, but do you and your team have the time and space to do it right? Reviewing the context before beginning to implement can throw up important considerations.

> **THINKING PROMPTS**
>
> - Why do your students need live modelling – what gaps are you trying to close?
> - Where are these gaps and how do you know they exist?
> - Is there capacity for a new school improvement initiative, or does something need to be deimplemented?
> - Are there existing pockets of good live modelling practice that can be amplified or act as a starting point?

An audit or review of your team's practice can help to answer a lot of these questions. Being professionally curious by using book looks, staff and student voice will be an excellent place to start. The thinking prompts above can form the basis of your enquiry and give you the information to make an informed decision on how to proceed.

Preparing – sweating the practicalities and the pedagogies

If the why outweighs the challenges and the project is to go ahead, there are new challenges that need to be considered before we begin to implement. Live modelling is supported by technology and that technology needs to be supported by furniture and classrooms to be most efficient. There are shortcuts available, but it is paramount that we are mindful and take shortcuts purposefully. Shortcuts add risk and if we are making a choice we are planning to mitigate those.

The practical

A whole school initiative of live modelling is going to be expensive. Equipping classrooms or staff with visualisers is one thing, but in the ideal world a standing desk will be beneficial and there will be inevitable cables that will need to be considered in regard to health and safety.

Using a must, should and could approach to the project will reveal what is really essential and what could be upgraded or built on in the future.

For example:

Must: a visualiser in every classroom of a predominantly written subject, cable safety solutions to remove risk of tripping or damage.

Should: raised surface for teachers to stand at – laptop stands.

Could: adjustable height standing desks for every classroom.

The financial side of a project such as this is a significant risk that must be considered and mitigated or it will never get off the ground. The investment in live modelling will improve standards when it is implemented well, also this is a one off cost, so looking into grants is another interesting opportunity.

> **THINKING PROMPTS**
>
> - What must you have, what should you have and what could you have?
> - How will this be funded?
> - How will you ensure that every classroom remains safe without wires acting as trip hazards?

The pedagogical

My personal belief is that live modelling is a game changing pedagogy for many students and having a whole school collective approach will make it easier for staff and students to adopt, however your school's context needs to be considered. However, teachers are like bookshelves, once they are full, you need to take something else off to add if you want it to stay organised and easy to navigate. Too many initiatives can very quickly become confusing and inevitably lead to busy teachers reverting to the processes they know and trust to make their lives and lessons easier. If a teacher is new to live modelling, they will drop it if they feel overwhelmed or unsupported in the process.

Also, reviewing wider contexts for your school is important. It is very hard to implement pedagogical improvements if there are behavioural issues that make teaching difficult. It might be that your responsibility is for teaching and learning, not behaviour, but the link between them is clear. Live modelling at a visualiser is a cognitively demanding task for a teacher and the effectiveness will diminish when teachers are having to concentrate on intensive behaviour management.

It is at this point that you need to consider what you want live modelling to look like in your school. What expectations are you going to set? There needs to be a balance in clarity and uniformity of approach with flexibility. Blanket pedagogical approaches such as: every lesson must contain live modelling, are doomed to fail, because for some subjects or parts of some subjects it is simply not appropriate or necessary. Whereas, woolly approaches without expectation will never take root in teachers' practice. How you balance this must be completely based on your unique school context.

A project such as this will have significant middle leader and staff training needs. Middle leaders need time and space to do the disciplinary work on what their process for structuring answers is, the progression model for how the good becomes great and how the skills of writing are integrated into the curriculum as it spirals.

Following this, there is value in middle leaders working interdisciplinarily to forge connections. For example, English and history may have similar sentence patterning in analytical paragraphs and geography and science might have joined approaches to writing a response to a graph, these could be integrated to ease uptake or delineated to protect the disciplinary literacy approaches for each subject. This is a decision that can be made on a case-by case-basis by the middle leaders. Understanding that there is an element of crossover between writing in subjects is important and helping students to understand these connections can help subjects nourish each other. Examples of these are connective words and phrases, which can be accepted on a whole school, faculty or multi department level. For example, graphs are present in maths, science and geography lessons, but the head of maths may point out that their graphs are used to provide information in a calculation, but the heads of geography and science use graphs more to extrapolate information and make inferences based on the data. The school may decide that the geography and science department develop a shared language and approach to graphs, but maths will have a separate approach.

Yourself and the middle leaders then need to train the staff on the processes of 'I do, we do, you do' from previous chapters and the good practice from the playbook chapter. Additionally, schemes of work may need to be adjusted to include opportunities for live modelling. This could be an external CPD approach, a twilight or PD day activity, but it needs to be given attention and time or it won't happen or won't happen well.

The EEF reminds us of the importance of engaging people "so they can shape what happens" and "unite people around what is being implemented". If it feels ad hoc or like a burden, staff are less likely to embrace the opportunity, no matter how powerful. Giving time to consider how it will be introduced to staff and giving them capacity to do it well couldn't be more important.

THINKING GUIDE

- Is your school context ready for an initiative of this type?
- Is there work to do around this project?
- What will live modelling look like in your school?
    - ☐ Will it differ by subjects
    - ☐ Will there be a base expectation for all staff or lessons?
    - ☐ What will be the same across the school?
    - ☐ What will be different across the school?
- How will you find time for middle leaders to think, research and plan?
- How will you find time to train staff well?

Delivering

With all of the thinking and preparing done, it is time to deliver. The roll out to teachers needs to happen on two levels: general and disciplinary.

The general training ranges from the simple how to use the visualiser and troubleshooting any small scale practical issues, to how to work through the stages of live modelling and delivering acceptable challenge for all learners.

The technical ability of your staff is likely to be inconsistent and some will be comfortable to plug it in and work it out, others will need support. This is easy to overlook, especially if you are very technologically literate yourself. The model of visualisers you are using will have their own troubleshooting guides and creating a series of common problems with simple fixes will save your IT team hours. Work with IT to identify the kinds of simple user fixable problems they are required to help with and address those issues as part of your CPD offer. Remove the barriers before they become barriers and the implementation process will be much simpler.

Pedagogical training should begin with the whole school elements and foci being introduced before disciplinary approaches can be secured by middle leaders and utilise opportunities for rehearsal the broader and more general structures that will translate across disciplines.

The initial launch can focus on communicating the why and the broad structures, but should focus upon the elements of writing that will be a whole school focus. Launching well builds buying draw attention to the benefits students will see from a staff body using a consistent approach and set of practices in a disciplinary way.

The strengthening of and focus on the disciplinary will help to build ownership and can be implemented immediately after training in classrooms using existing pedagogies that teachers are confident with. It empowers middle leaders to take ownership of the project and oils the wheels with some 'quick-wins' that will kick start the project by beginning to improve the teaching of writing. Once this has occurred, it gives teachers a foundation on which to build live modelling into their practice. Confident teachers of their subject will be better live modellers and confidence comes from the clarity of approach. Teachers benefit from clear direction too because teaching is such a cognitively demanding task.

Once teachers feel confident in teaching writing within their subject, the quality of their live modelling practice can be influenced by a CPD on a whole school or faculty level. This can return to the focus of 'I do, we do and you do' and utilise modelling or video to allow staff to see it happening and focus on the processes to translate into their own classroom.

> **THINKING PROMPTS**
>
> - How can you communicate your why to motivate and enthuse?
> - What are the core elements of the why that need to be clear?
> - How will you link the whole school and disciplinary live modelling?
> - What is the balance you want to strike between compliance with a whole school policy and departmental freedom?
> - What will compliance look like on a whole school, departmental and individual teacher level?

Sustain: keep the success going

The hardest part of implementation is the same as learning: making it stick. So many school improvement initiatives fail with the phrase: "we're already doing that". You might have done it, but to be able to use the present tense verb requires a clear and coordinated approach to both monitoring and maintaining.

Monitoring is a scary concept for many teachers. Even the most secure workplaces are likely to have an element of nervousness about a member of SLT appearing on a learning walk and there is a balance to be struck between seeing the reality of a student's daily diet by arriving unannounced and considering staff wellbeing with a planned visit. Additionally, it can go beyond visiting lessons on a learning walk and should be present in book looks, student and staff voice.

As a leader, you need to know what's going on in your school and the purpose of live modelling focussed monitoring is to review the effectiveness of application and levels of compliance among the staff. Specifically you need to identify misconceptions and lethal mutations.

Misconceptions are missed opportunities in lessons or misapplications of the processes, they are caused by errors or minor misunderstandings. In previous chapters we have discussed the value in breaking the cycle of 'I do, we do you do' with purpose to maximise learning and respond to a class's needs. Rigidity can be brittle and a teacher marching through the stages without pausing to assess readiness and comprehension and a teacher missing steps out or going through the motions could both be based upon a misconception of how the process of live modelling could and should be applied. Identifying the misconceptions and addressing them on a one-to-one or a whole staff level is vital to successfully sustaining not just live modelling, but any school improvement initiative.

Lethal mutations are more concerning because they are ingrained and much harder to root out, they are serious misunderstandings of what something is and what it needs to be effective. If your monitoring is strong, then they should not happen regularly, but you must still be aware of them. An example of a lethal mutation is a teacher using the 'I do' phase as a pure copying exercise without doing the work around thought narration or routine building: students become passive and no learning is taking place. Progress will stall or stop completely as the 'I do' makes the process inaccessible instead of demystifying it.

These lethal mutations must be addressed quickly and clearly. The longer they go on, the harder they are to remove and the more likely they are to spread. Or, one teacher's lack of success can reduce their motivation and lead to the benefits being lost.

Compliance is a bit of a dirty word in education, but there is a level where good teaching is just good teaching and aligning a teaching staff with some of them in an organised fashion is the simplest way to have a massive impact on the lives of a large number of students. Compliance is not a stick to beat people with, it's a way of ensuring that every student gets the best diet of education every day. There is a line at which compliance can become a flattening force that forgets that different lessons and teachers don't fit into a cookie cutter lesson rubric, but don't be afraid to seek points of the process that you expect to be echoed as a shared standard.

Monitoring is vitally important and if you are trying to do it alone it will lose potency. You don't have capacity to quality assure a whole staff body in detail with a single focus. Building a team around you and leveraging the resources you have available is the most powerful thing that you can do. Training middle leaders on what you want them to look for and maintaining a focus on high quality feedback from their observations of lessons, books and student voice will give you a wealth of information that you can plough into maintaining.

Maintaining requires that every member of the teaching team is 'up to date' and onboard. Live modelling needs to be a permanent fixture in your CPD offer, best practice needs to be amplified, misconceptions managed and lethal mutations challenged.

The CPD offer at your school must reflect your shared vision and link back to your why. It is vastly more complex than rerunning the CPD sessions or running them for new members of the teaching staff. It needs to be adaptive and responsive to the areas, positive and negative, that your monitoring systems throw up and any other threats, such as different school improvement initiatives from the pressure to always be doing something new and different.

The balance comes between not resting on your laurels and not banging the same drum over and over again. One of the best ways to do this is amplifying best practice. Recording your best live modellers or inviting them to lead CPD can bring fresh ideas and voices to reinvigorate the project, not to mention building up your team to be proud of the work they do in the classroom.

THINKING PROMPTS

- What is important for you to monitor?
- How will you amass data and sift through it to identify best practice, misconceptions and lethal mutations?
- What does compliance mean to you and the school in regard to this project?
- Who can you utilise to monitor effectively?
- How often will you offer top up CPD to existing staff?
- How will you 'onboard' new teachers to the school?
- How can you share best practice within your school?

Reference

Jonathan Sharples, Jon Eaton and Jamila Boughelaf, A School's Guide to Implementation, The Education Endowment Foundation Guidance Reports. Accessed 8th September 2024, https://educationendowmentfoundation.org.uk/education-evidence/guidance-reports/implementation

9 The playbook

This section is a culmination of strategies and learning routines that have a range of different opportunities for use across the curriculum. Experiment and find what works for you and your learners.

Double width margins

Description:

Students use a ruler to make their margin twice as wide.

This space is used to capture prompts, ideas and snippets of expertise in the 'I do'.

These notes provide scaffolding for the 'we and you dos'.

Ideas for application:

1. You model the answer and make process notes to make your thought narration more concrete.
2. Students focus on your thought narration and capture notes only as you model.
3. You guide them through setting up the margin notes as a step by step and use them as a class in the 'we do'
4. The margin becomes an assessment space after the 'you do' for reflective note taking and target setting.
5. The margin is filled with a printed banner to scaffold very clearly without the need to write from the board.

Strengths:

- Maximises the perception of writing as a step-by-step process.
- Easily scales with growing expertise.
- Can be adapted with relative ease.
- Flexible for use in different ways.
- Easily trainable as a routine.

Limitations:

- Requires student motivation to capture the notes.
- Student notes may be inconsistent and mask misconceptions.

Double spaced lines

Description:

The model is captured with a blank line to double space the work.

The model can be annotated and labelled after it has been written.

Ideas:

1. Write the model double spacing with the class and annotate it as a 'we do'.
2. Give the students the model and go through it granularly and they can capture the specific choices in annotation.
3. Use highlighters or different colour pens to identify patterned expert choices.

Strengths:

- Makes clear links to success criteria and makes those criteria explicit.
- Excellent for highlighting specific decisions that are used often, e.g. connective phrases.

Limitations:

- Requires student motivation.
- Students making unguided annotations may make inconsistent quality reflections or include misconceptions.

Show calling

Description:

After the 'you do', select student work that exemplifies good practice of the specific criteria.

Place that work under the visualiser and mark it or discuss it as a class.

Ideas:

1. Mark a students work 'live' in front of the class, making links across the 'I do, you do we do' stages.
2. Mark student work as an examiner to draw in assessment objectives or mark schemes.
3. Students can come to the visualiser and narrate their writing

Strengths:

- Builds student motivation.
- Students see that the expert approach is achievable.
- It is an opportunity to catch students who struggle doing the right thing.
- Students can be marked for different criterion and misconceptions can be addressed as well as successes.
- Enhances reflective approaches and a willingness to edit and improve.

Limitations:

- Students may be unwilling to share their work or narrate it if the culture isn't right.
- It is important to use a range of students.

Intentional mistakes and non-examples

Description:

During the 'I do' stage, intentional mistakes and misconceptions are included.

These are then performatively noticed and corrected.

Ideas:

1. Mirror the misconceptions that you have noticed to show them why it is incorrect and how to fix it.
2. Write a bad model and use the 'we do' to improve it.
3. Use it as part of a feedback sequence and students use the 'you do' to redraft their own work.

Strengths:

- Allows for spot removal of errors.
- Helps students to identify their own mistakes and gives a framework to correct it.
- Builds a culture of reflection and editing.

Limitations:

- Serious misconceptions need to be retaught and require greater attention than this approach.

Teaching planning

Description:

Moving live modelling to the step before writing, by modelling planning.

Using a grid style plan, the stages of live modelling can each be used to fill in a box on the grid.

Ideas:

1. Students complete the first box with you, work together on the second two and complete the last independently.
2. This can lead into a writing sequence where the final paragraph is completely organic having been planned and written by the student.

Strengths:

- Underpins a vital, yet overlooked skill.
- Builds expertise around thinking in addition to writing.
- Allows the approach you want to teach to be scaffolded with a carefully phased plan that will support writing independently.
- Makes students more likely to plan in fully independent tasks, improving quality of writing.

Limitations:

- Students need to have adequate knowledge to plan – this is not a powerful way to teach content.
- Focuses on how knowledge can be translated into a writing task.

Reading annotation

Description:

Using specific general and disciplinary strategies explicitly to teach expert approaches to reading.

Students observe the expert reader, work with a peer and then complete the reading independently where appropriate.

Ideas:

1. Skim and scan – show how to quickly move your eyes over the words looking for terminology, challenging vocabulary or words identified by the writer [E.G. in bold]. Scan any supporting information such as images or diagrams.
2. Predict – Explore what you believe this text might be about or how it might fit into your existing knowledge base.
3. Criteria for reading – set criteria of what is going to be identified, highlighted or sought out.
4. Tools for reading – review strategies for focus [E.G. ruler reading].
5. Question and clarify – Build in pauses during reading to check your own understanding and identify if a reread is necessary. Pause over key vocabulary or points to clarify meaning.
6. Summarise – Consider how this reading has illuminated or challenged your current understanding. Identify the most salient points from the reading.

Strengths:

- Builds strategic reading skills, which underpin thinking and writing like an expert by providing information to form ideas.
- A strong culture of reading in a school will nourish every single subject and the life chances of every student.

Limitations:

- Requires clear expectations at each step.
- Sources must be appropriately challenging and presented in an appropriate manner for students to access.

What would be better?

Description:

During the 'I do' or 'we do' pause after writing something that could be improved and ask, "what would be better?"

Students can stop, discuss and suggest.

Ideas:

1. Use to teach specific vocabulary or to broaden student's vocabulary.
2. Require students to explain their suggestions with a defence of why their option will improve the piece.

Strengths:

- Provides opportunities to model expert reflection.
- Reinforces links to the success criteria in writing.
- Breaks up modelling to allow for student reflection.

Limitations:

- Students must understand what they are suggesting and why they are suggesting it – otherwise they are just guessing.

The shared blank page

Description:

A fully live lesson where each task is introduced on the visualiser by the teacher writing tasks and scaffolds as they are required.

The planning is completed carefully, but not visible in regard to a slide show, etc.

Ideas:

1. Plan your lesson carefully in regard to learning and activities.
2. Use your formative assessment skills to react to student need by adding scaffolding as needed.

Strengths:

- Allows teaching to be fully responsive to the needs of the students.
- Flexibility on what is explored and how much support is given.
- Teaches students how to lay out their work.

Limitations:

- Can be challenging for the cognitive load of the teacher.
- Requires strong subject knowledge and routines to be established.

Bibliography

Judith Hochman and Natalie Wexler, *The Writing Revolution* (San Francisco: Jossey-Bass, 2017), 40.

Kate Jones (2023). The Curse of Knowledge: A Cognitive Bias All Teachers Should Be Aware of, Evidence Based Education. Accessed 8th September 2024, https://evidencebased.education/the-curse-of-knowledge-a-cognitive-bias-all-teachers-should-be-aware-of/

Mary Kennedy (2016). How Does Professional Development Improve Teaching? *Review of Educational Research*. Accessed 8th September 2024, https://doi.org/10.3102/0034654315626800

Peps Mccrea (2020), *Motivated Teaching*.

Avnee Morjaria, The Oxford Language Report 2023–2024: Highlights for Schools. Accessed 8th September 2024, https://fdslive.oup.com/www.oup.com/oxed/wordgap/Oxford_Language_Report_2023-24_Building_Vocabulary_At_School.pdf?region=international

Jan Plass, Roxana Morena and Roland Brunken, *Cognitive Load Theory* (New York: Cambridge University Press, 2010), 17.

Alex Quigley, *Closing the Reading Gap* (Abingdon: Routledge, 2020), 15.

Alex Quigley and Robbie Coleman, Improving Literacy in Secondary Schools. Accessed 8th September 2024, https://d2tic4wvo1iusb.cloudfront.net/production/eef-guidance-reports/literacy-ks3-ks4/EEF_KS3_KS4_LITERACY_GUIDANCE.pdf?v=1725803331

Alex Quigley, Grammar moves for Academic Writing. Accessed 21st February, 2025, https://alexquigley.co.uk/content/images/wordpress/2022/05/CTWG-Top-10-grammar-moves-poster.pdf

Recording SEN and Medical Categories Guidance for Schools: January 2019. Accessed 9th September 2024, https://www.education-ni.gov.uk/sites/default/files/publications/education/SEN%20and%20Medical%20Categories%20Guidance%20-%20January%202019_4.pdf

Index

academic reading 31
accountable feedback 54
adaptations 67, 68
annotation 8, 48, 81
apathy 20
attention 47; building buy-in and making it matter 19–20; power of 19
Autistic Spectrum conditions (ASC) 65, 66

behaviour management 53
blanket pedagogical approaches 72
BUG 22

chunking reading 32
cognitive load 9, 19, 22, 40, 43, 47; criteria to direct student attention and manage 56; profound importance 66–68; self-scaffolding 47; on students and teachers 17; vocabulary 31
collaboration: high dependency stage of 51; at levels of expertise 52
compliance 76
CPD 73, 74, 76

decision-making 17, 18, 22, 68, 70
dictation 53, 55
disciplinary approaches, teacher training 74
disciplinary literacy 27
double spaced lines 43, 44, 79
double width margins 43–44, 47, 67, 78
dyslexia 65–66

Education Endowment Foundation (EEF) 27, 70, 73; school guide to implementation 70
English literature 37
expertise: curse of 28; difference between knowledge and 13
experts: curse of 37, 38; level of 51; read 27–28
extended writing 9, 20, 38, 57
extraneous loads 17–19

feedback 61; forms of 60–61
five Ws 32
fluency, reading 32–33
formative assessment 50; using live marking as 59–60
formative feedback 61
Frayer model 30

GCSE exams 20
general training, teachers 74
germane load 17, 18
'greatness criteria' 44, 46

Hochman's approach 60

'I do' modelling 9, 14, 59, 60; reading 27–35 (*see also* reading); writing 36–48 (*see also* writing)
inclusion, juggling act of 65
inclusive live modelling 65–69
intentional mistakes and non-examples 45, 80

interactivity 19
intrinsic load 17

knowing *vs.* doing 13
knowledge 9, 54; collective 22; curse of 2; difference between expertise and 2, 13; and skills 70

learners: apathetic 20; novice nature of 30
learning: moderate learning difficulties 65, 66; overlearning 68; specific goals and 43; specific learning difficulty 65, 66
learning sequences 46
lethal mutations 75–76
live marking 60–61
live modelling 7, 49–50; benefits of 8–9; building conditions for 17–22; delivering 74–75; inclusive 65–69; limitation of 8–9, 61; pace of 20–22; pedagogical 12–16, 72–73; physical 10–12; practical 71; routines for (*see* routines); stage for learners with SEN 68; sustaining 75–77; thinking and implementation guide 70–77

Mccrea, Peps: *Motivated Teaching* 19
middle leaders 72, 73, 76
mind mapping 11
misconceptions 42–44, 46, 75; monitoring for 57–58; profundity of 59
moderate learning difficulties (MLD) 65, 66
monitoring 75, 76; for misconceptions 57–58
Motivated Teaching (Mccrea) 19
motivation 9, 14, 20, 47; to meet expectations 53–54; micro-elements in 20–22; power of 19
"moves" 21

non-fiction reading 29
novice: acquisition of expertise 1; cognitive load 40; nature of learners 30; problem-solving/extended writing task 9

oracy 53
overlearning 68

pathetic fallacy 13–16
pedagogical, live modelling 12; objectives and desirable elements 12–13; practicalities and 71; step-by-step method of teaching 13–16; training 74
peer assessment 60–61
phrase banks 67
popcorn reading 32
praise 19
problem-solving/extended writing task 9
pronunciation, reading 32–33
prosody, reading 32–33

Quigley, Alex 21, 27

reading 27–28; annotation 81; clarifying and questioning 34; experts 27–28; fluency, prosody and pronunciation 32–33; knowing your purpose 31–32; skills explicit to ourselves 28–30; stages of 33–34; summarise and synthesise 34; vocabulary 30–31
reciprocal reading strategies 33
Rosenshine, B. 7
routines: automaticity through 18; design element 18–19; importance of 17–18; power of 22; structured oracy 53

scanning 34
script lead-ins 18–19
self-assessment 60–61
self-esteem 9, 14, 20
self-scaffolding 47–48
SEN 65, 66, 68
sentence starters 67
Shakespeare, W. 41–42, 44, 45
shared blank page 82
show-calling 43, 60–61, 79
skimming 33
SPaG errors 44, 45
specific learning difficulty (SpLD) 65, 66
static model 7; limitations and benefits of 8–9
step-by-step 'flowchart' type approach 50
step-by-step modelling 38
stripey writing 60

student-led reading 32
students: with ASC 66; chunking reading 32; clarity of purpose 54; cognitive load on 17; collecting responses, bouncing and refining 54–55; with dyslexia 66; as editors 55; high dependency level 51–52; in KS3 33; in KS5 33; lower dependency level 53; with MLD 66; motivation 9; need of opportunities 56; selecting and presenting reading to 33; self-esteem 9, 20; with SEN 66, 68; with SpLD 66; support to rejoin dots 58–59
Suffolk Dyslexia Specialist Teaching Team 68
summative feedback 61

task trackers 67
teacher models sentence 60
teachers: cognitive load on 17; training for 74
teaching: planning 80; step-by-step method of 13–16
thought narration 42, 47, 48
three-page grade 7 literature essay 8
typing onto a document approach, pros and cons 10

visualisers 11–12, 71, 72; pros and cons 10; reciprocal reading strategies 33
vocabulary 30–31, 67
vocabulary gap 30
vocational activities 8–9

WAGOLL (what a good one looks like) 7–9
'we do' process 9, 14, 49, 68; clarity of purpose 54; collecting students responses, bouncing and refining 54–55; identifying when we can do 50; levels of dependence 50–53
whiteboard approach 10; pros and cons 11
whole class feedback system 61
whole school collective approach 72
working memory 17
writing 36–38; annotate 48; effective and high-level disciplinary process for 66; good to great 43–46; if i write it, you write it 47; rules of 36, 37; self-scaffolding 47–48; staircase, not a slope 38–43; students teaching 46–47

'you do' process 9, 14, 49; attempting independence 55–56; criteria to direct student 56–57; show-calling 60–61

For Product Safety Concerns and Information please contact our EU representative GPSR@taylorandfrancis.com
Taylor & Francis Verlag GmbH, Kaufingerstraße 24, 80331 München, Germany